HIGHER EDUCATION IN THE GULF STATES

Other Titles in the Series

SOAS MIDDLE EAST ISSUES

Higher Education in the Gulf States:
Shaping Economies, Politics and Culture

Edited by

Christopher Davidson & Peter Mackenzie Smith

SAQI

in association with

**LONDON
MIDDLE EAST
INSTITUTE
SOAS**

ISBN: 978-0-86356-697-4

© London Middle East Institute at SOAS, 2008

A full CIP record for this book is available from the British Library.

A full CIP record for this book is available from the Library of Congress.

Manufactured in Lebanon

SAQI

26 Westbourne Grove, London W2 5RH
825 Page Street, Suite 203, Berkeley, California 94710
Tabet Building, Mneimneh Street, Hamra, Beirut
www.saqibooks.com

in association with

The London Middle East Institute
School of Oriental and African Studies, Russell Square, London WC1H 0XG
www.lmei.soas.ac.uk

Contents

Acknowledgments

This book has its origins in a conference organised by the London Middle East Institute (LMEI) of the School of Oriental and African Studies (SOAS) in November 2007 under the title 'Higher Education in the GCC States: building economies, societies and nations'. The conference was attended by a wide range of academics and practitioners for the Gulf region, for whose enthusiasm and support we are very grateful. This volume, which is based on its proceedings, is intended to bring the topic to a wider audience.

The conference could not have gone ahead without sponsorship. The London Middle East Institute wishes to acknowledge the generous support of the MBI Al Jaber Foundation, the Embassy of the State of Qatar, MENAS Associates, Research Analysts, the British Council, Gulf States Newsletter and Curtis, Mallet-Prevost, Colt & Mosle LLP.

This is the seventh book in the SOAS Middle East Issues series published by Saqi in association with the LMEI. The editors wish to acknowledge the assistance provided by Louise Hosking of the LMEI and by Shikha Sethi and Lara Frankena of Saqi Books.

Introduction

Peter Mackenzie Smith

This book derives from the contributions and discussions held at the conference 'Higher Education in the GCC States: building economies, societies and nations', which was organised by the London Middle East Institute of the School of Oriental and African Studies in London in November 2007. They are supplemented by additional material considered by the organisers as being relevant to the theme and arising from discussion sessions at the conference.

The rationale for the conference was that it was appropriate to consider at this time the rapid expansion of higher education in the six member countries of the Gulf Cooperation Council (GCC) and to review the ways in which each country was designing and implementing this expansion and the reform programmes that underpin it. Each country is pursuing its own route in developing tertiary education, but there are common trends and themes which the conference sought to identify and share. This introduction seeks to reflect these common considerations and to examine their manifestations in the individual countries of the GCC.

No review of the current higher education systems in the Gulf countries should ignore the definitive World Bank development report, *The Road not Traveled*, published by the Bank in early 2008. A digest and commentary of the report's findings by Mari Luomi are therefore part of this volume. Its main conclusion, which covers all

levels of education in the Middle East and North Africa, is that the
education systems in the region require a new approach to reform,
based on an emphasis on public accountability and incentives and on
seeking to close the gap between the supply of educated individuals
and both internal and external labour demand. These two principal
strands appear to a greater or lesser degree in most of the contributions
to this book, albeit under different headings. This is perhaps best
reflected in the emphasis on the development of independent quality
assurance systems in almost all the countries involved and on the
awareness of the need for greater relevance of equipping graduates
with skills and capabilities more in tune with the requirements of
business, industry and the world of employment, both within the
region and on an international level.

The main themes in higher education in the region that emerge
from this book, generally illustrated from experience and observation
in individual countries, are:

- Expansion from a small historical base,
- Access to higher education and the issue of gender,
- Quality and accountability,
- International links and partnerships,
- Meeting private and public sector employment needs,
- Nationalisation of the labour force, especially in the
  smaller Gulf states.

All these areas are interlinked, with some cross-cutting dimensions
which touch upon each. So, for example, most Gulf universities and
colleges interact with partner institutions in Europe, North America
and Australia or are branches of them, as in the case illustrated by the
chapter on the British University in Dubai, and these relationships have
assumed profound importance for all aspects of tertiary education. A
cross-cutting theme, emphasised by the World Bank and by other contributors, is the impact on the institutions of the region of globalisation
in general and of the desire to create knowledge economies in particular.
Another cross-cutting theme is the extent to which states should cater
for the educational needs of their expatriate communities.

Expansion and History

Christopher Davidson's chapter provides an important reminder of the origins of educational development in the Gulf and of the remarkable fact that, apart from in Saudi Arabia, the first ministries of education in the region were only established in the early 1970s, following the British withdrawal. He traces the origins of basic and secondary education and the roles played by the merchants of the region and by neighbouring Arab states in setting up the first schools following what he describes as a period of neglect under the British. He notes the transition from religious to secular schools, the establishment of specific schools for girls, the use of overseas scholarships as the initiator for higher education, and the impact of these developments on the traditional societies of the region. His chapter also reminds us that, until as late as the early 1960s, some of the countries of the region had not yet begun significant development of their oil and gas resources and relied heavily on other Arab countries for financial as well as educational support. Thus emerging institutions originally relied on predominantly Egyptian and Palestinian teachers both for teaching and for curriculum development and on Kuwait in particular for financial support. Although the public purses of the Gulf countries might now be said to be more than sufficient for domestic purposes, the tendency to import teaching and education management expertise has remained until today.

Gregory Starrett's chapter widens the historical view to the origins of modern higher education in the Ottoman Empire, particularly Turkey, Egypt and Iraq. He also introduces the concept that schools and universities need to be seen as engines of change, development and progress in their societies and that this brings with it the risk of instability. Noting that the ministries of education across the region are now adept at using the international language of management, policy and strategy development, he raises the perennial questions of the purposes of higher education and whether universities should be 'corporate bodies of faculty which decide the nature of the curriculum and of their own research programmes' or commercial corporations run along modern management lines with their own criteria for success. While his general conclusion is that education can effectively be all things to all people, he cautions that higher education should not be constantly aimed at the 'whims of the market'. Starrett's chapter offers insights on the leadership and inspirational and charismatic role he sees both individuals and institutions playing through education. His views challenge those responsible for higher education development in the region to balance carefully their objectives for institutions of higher education.

The expansion from this base forty years ago to the provision of all levels of education within the region in the early twenty-first century has been dramatic. The chapters in this book illustrate the achievements of the region in establishing and developing new universities and tertiary colleges at a remarkable rate. They also describe the population growth rates and the challenges that all the Gulf states face in meeting the needs and aspirations of their very youthful populations.

Access to Higher Education and the Issue of Gender

The principal contributions in this volume on access and gender are by Warren Fox and Jane Bristol-Rhys. Both look in detail at the experience of the United Arab Emirates, but the theme is a general one, with greater detail in terms of facts and figures for the region available in the World Bank report.

Fox describes the achievements of the UAE in tertiary education and highlights the paradox of higher education in a country seeking to build a knowledge economy yet undergoing a funding crisis in investment programmes in this sector, which are currently well below international comparators. His account covers the complexity of a federal strategic planning process that is being initiated against a backdrop of ongoing, individual emirate-level actions, especially in Dubai. He reveals that while the public sector may be facing funding constraints, the private sector is not. The pattern of new developments includes an expanding 'national university' at Al-'Ayn (where 70 per cent of the student body are women), new colleges of higher education and a number of private universities, including many accredited by foreign institutions (for example the Sorbonne and the New York Institute of Technology in Abu Dhabi) and the sixteen branch campuses of foreign universities operating from within the Dubai Knowledge Village. The opportunities for higher education for UAE nationals, both male and female, and for expatriate students have consequently greatly increased, although significant constraints remain evident. Many male UAE nationals, for example, have not completed high school and often seek alternative employment in the public sector or in family businesses.

Bristol-Rhys describes the way in which this expansion has resulted in many more gender-mixed campuses, especially in the private education sector. Gender-integrated public sector institutions conduct separate classes for men and women. She points out that women are now in the majority among students of public sector institutions and that their participation in the labour force is increasing. She tempers these observations, however, by describing the social constraints under which women live in a patriarchal society. The overall picture is of a higher education system which is increasingly developing through public and private sector engagement to meet the demand of its nationals, and, to some extent, its expatriate population, with the qualification that demotivated males continue to seek alternatives to higher education while females take greater advantage of educational opportunities, but face discrimination in the labour market.

Quality and Accountability

A recurrent theme in the following chapters is how to improve and measure the quality of higher education offered by both public and private higher education institutions in the Gulf. The impetus for this desire both to upgrade and to evaluate tertiary education is grounded in the concern that the qualifications and experience of students graduating from Gulf institutions should be of an international standard, for the global competitiveness of the countries concerned depends on the knowledge and competence of their youth. The higher education strategies of the Gulf countries all stress the need for quality assurance systems. The route that most endorse is of emulating those systems that presently operate in Western Europe and North America. International comparison, coupled with a greater accountability in the management and provision of education is, in fact, the basis of the World Bank's proposals for education reform, which are also reflected in the following chapters. Achieving globally competitive quality is the rationale for many of the partnerships established with international university partners, either as branches or as various forms of joint venture. Public sector higher education institutions in the Gulf are also more open to collaborative ventures with foreign universities than has been the case in the past and the notion of international benchmarks has gained greater acceptance in that sector as well.

The development of a regional solution to quality assurance is a growing concern. Moudi al-Humoud's chapter reflects this, as it proposes a regional quality assurance agency to monitor standards in each country and to issue academic awards. Her approach is based on methodologies and practices developed by the UK's Quality Assurance Agency over the past ten years. Her proposal covers both public and private universities, as well as other degree awarding institutions. She reveals that the adoption of the British model was initially opposed in academic circles, but has now gained acceptance as a necessary and helpful system. Some of the Gulf states have preferred to develop their own national agencies and systems. Khalil al-Khalili's chapter describes the situation in Bahrain, where the education strategy recently adopted through the Economic Development Board provides for the establishment of a home-grown quality assurance authority which will have inspection units for universities, vocational education colleges and schools, and will supervise all examinations. It is intended to be an independent government entity that will cooperate with the Australian Universities Quality Agency until it develops its own capacities. The chapters on quality assurance note in addition that an enhanced quality assurance and accountability system would provide to the public more information on the performance of higher education institutions than is presently the case in most of the Gulf countries. This in turn would improve the quality of individual decision-making about educational choices and provide a basis for macro level assessments of progress within the education system.

International Links and Partnerships

The extent to which higher education in the Gulf countries is increasingly linked to international experience and provision is an essential element in its maturation. The earliest developments in higher education in the region involved overseas scholarships within the Arab world and in the West. Most of the current generation of the Gulf's higher education managers received all or part of their own higher education at foreign universities, often in Egypt or in the West. International faculty dominated the initial higher education institutions and remain an important component of the teaching faculty across the region. More recent pressures for reform have come from the globalised economy, initially in the oil and gas industry and subsequently in other areas such as finance, so the current drivers for improved quality, access and provision are now the demands to equip graduates to be internationally competitive. This is, of course, not solely a Gulf concern, for all in higher education are aware of international pressures and comparisons.

Projects to establish universities are proliferating throughout the GCC. The nature of these projects varies: some are set up as branches of their overseas institutions, some as partnerships between Gulf institutions and overseas collaborators. Most are in the private sector and at the undergraduate level. Perhaps the best-known example is the cluster of institutions participating in Dubai Knowledge Village, where institutions from Australia, India, Russia, Canada, Pakistan, Belgium and the UK have set up campuses. In addition to specific projects for the development of new institutions, or branches of existing ones, overseas universities are now more active in seeking teaching and research links with Gulf institutions across a wide spectrum of subject areas. In some cases these links provide for Gulf students and faculty to spend part of their studies overseas, for faculty exchanges and joint research programmes. One of the outcomes of establishing quality assurance agencies as described above could be to enhance this process and encourage the development of easier exchange of qualifications and standards, in research as well as in teaching.

David Lock's chapter describes the origins and development of one specific international institution, the British University in Dubai. This project – to establish a postgraduate university – is also an excellent example of a partnership between industry and educational institutions, with the original initiative coming from British and UAE business concerns. Lock describes the way in which five UK universities were brought together to offer masters programmes in Dubai in a range of subjects relevant to the economic needs of the UAE, and to engage in research in these areas. The emphasis has been on delivering degrees in Dubai that will be equivalent to those offered by the UK universities at their home campuses, and on engendering research activity.

Digby Swift's chapter outlines what he sees as the potential contribution of Gulf universities to international development, a logical progression of this internationalising agenda. Swift argues that universities, in addition to their roles in support of their students, research and local economies and societies, have a wider duty to the international community in reducing global deprivation and strengthening global understanding and partnership. He takes the view that GCC universities, juxtaposed between East and West, generally well equipped and operating in a region of rapid change and expanding economies with excellent international links and connections, are well placed to open up access to students from poorer countries. They should establish projects and programmes in support of wider engagement with international development. He quotes examples of the kind of collaborations that are already effective in addressing these tasks and suggests more detailed consideration of these roles in current higher education planning in the region.

As a complement to this proposal, Ali al-Shamlan sets out in his chapter the background and activities of the Kuwait Foundation for the Advancement of Sciences, which invests in projects in support of scientific and other endeavours both nationally and internationally and works closely with higher education institutions. Al-Shamlan describes the KFAS's investment policies and programmes since its establishment in 1976. The Foundation supports a wide range of projects for scientific infrastructure, institutional research, technical innovation, skills development and international collaboration. Its activities include the funding of chairs, centres of excellence and research grants at Kuwaiti and international universities. In addition to scientific and medical subject areas, the Foundation is also engaged in projects in leadership, public strategy and policy development, Islamic studies, heritage conservation and management and information studies. It has contributed to international development programmes in the developing world and supports a number of libraries and information centres at institutions in Kuwait and overseas. The work of the Foundation can perhaps be seen as the modern extension of earlier Kuwaiti investments in educational development in the region in the 1960s and 1970s, which Christopher Davidson records in his chapter.

Relevance to Employment and the Labour Market

A recurring theme in the World Bank report concerns the perceived mismatch between the labour market and the output of the education systems of the Gulf, as well as those of the wider Middle East and North Africa region. Each of the declared strategies of the Gulf countries for higher education addresses the need for universities and colleges to equip graduates for the labour market and the world of work and to contribute to the economic development of their countries. Several countries have in place policies for the replacement of their expatriate populations by an effective national workforce and most are concerned with the need to develop industries and businesses outside the dominant energy sector. The implicit common strategy is that each country should be able to compete globally on the basis, among other things, of having an effective, efficient and innovative private sector to which indigenous higher educational institutions are linked.

Many of the older, and some of the newer, universities in the region have been slow to initiate curriculum reform or to have considered how best to include programmes and relationships that will help graduates prepare for employment. There are also concerns about student competence in vocationally relevant areas such as mathematics and English, and about the 'core skills' (for example communication, presentation, team-working and working disciplines) which many employers now look for from new employees in most skill areas. These deficiencies are found in both male and female students, an issue that is particularly serious in the Gulf. The description of the foundation and development of the British University in Dubai in Lock's chapter illustrates one aspect of the way in which business and industry in the region have collaborated to try to develop a cadre of graduates with relevant experience of areas attractive to specific businesses. It is, however, a small and necessarily highly selective institution and does not have broad impact. The implications of the evidence presented in this volume and in the World Bank report are that the issue of linkage between universities and the labour market requires much more attention within the region.

Mohammed Alkhozai's chapter provides an excellent example of the way in which the introduction of new industries in the Gulf, in this case banking and finance, lead to the establishment of specialised institutes to provide education and training. The private sector Bahrain Institute of Banking and Finance offers a range of international qualifications in the field and works with a number of British and American academic and strategic partners in delivering to Bahraini and other GCC students courses and tailored programmes for the industry. It also delivers training in other GCC countries and includes general professional development programmes, such as leadership and management, in its offerings. Other examples of this type of institution include the long-established Petroleum Institute in Abu Dhabi, a collaborative venture with the Abu Dhabi National Oil Company and international oil company partners, and the Saudi British Electronic Institute in Riyadh, an initiative of BAE Systems. Industry relationships with education can be strong, particularly in the energy sector. Saudi

Aramco's work with the King Fahd University of Petroleum and Minerals is perhaps the longest established example. Nevertheless, many companies, businesses and chambers of commerce continue to complain that the products of schools, colleges and universities in the region require extensive additional education and training by their new employers before they become effective in the workplace.

Mari Luomi's analysis of the World Bank report reminds us that the UNDP's *Arab Human Development Report* of 2003 concentrated on the role of knowledge in development in the Middle East region. Its concept of an Arab knowledge model for the future considered the need for much greater transparency of educational structures, quality of education, science and research and knowledge-based production and services. The aspirations of all the GCC countries to create knowledge economies are repeated in the World Bank report. André Mazawi's chapter reflects on the way in which large-scale new developments in private sector higher education provision in the region (Dubai Knowledge Village, Qatar's Education City and many internationally connected new institutions in all countries) are said to be directed at meeting this demand, but run the risk of making the GCC countries consumers, rather than producers, in the knowledge economy.

The relationship between higher education and the human capital needs of economies, now and in future, is a challenge across the world. The contributions to this book illustrate some of the ways in which the GCC countries are seeking to meet it, but it is clear that there is a long way to go and that the GCC countries face particular obstacles, including gender relations, large expatriate populations, attitudes to employment and a predilection amongst graduates for the public sector. These challenges go to the heart of the overall theme of this book – the role of higher education in building economies, societies and nations. Mazawi's chapter in particular investigates intersections between culture, religion and politics in higher education reform in the region and emphasises the challenge of finding effective solutions where international models are at the core of educational systems. He deals in detail with the way in which post-school education in the region, with the potential exception of Saudi Arabia, is largely conducted through Western international linkages and accreditation systems, reinforced by the recruitment of increasing numbers of nationals of the region as faculty, who are themselves products either of international institutions or of their local partners in the Gulf. He also asks us to consider the political and developmental impact of these relationships on the societies of the region and on the associated economic policies of their governments. In this context Mazawi notes the role being played by the private sector, almost exclusively with Western partners, in almost every new educational initiative in the region, both in the development of institutions and in associated areas, like science parks and enterprise incubators. He sets out the implications of these developments in fairly stark terms, with much concern about the space available for home-grown influences or options within the overall expansion of higher education and the effect this weakness will have on national policies and character. He also argues for greater regional collaborative efforts, despite some disappointing examples so far, and for consideration of a GCC 'academic region' to enhance exchange and opportunity amongst both faculty and the graduates of the current national systems, with stronger links with the wider Arab world as well as internationally. He is keen to place the expansion of higher education in its developmental and social context, with particular attention to its potential impact on the political structures and philosophies of the region.

Conclusions, Issues and Challenges

The interconnection between higher education and economic and social development in the countries of the region is well illustrated in the varied contributions to this book that record the extraordinary expansion of higher education in the region since the establishment of the first universities (King Saud University in Riyadh in 1957 and the University of Kuwait in 1966) and which take up directly and indirectly the key issues related to this phenomenal growth. The region may have, or be in the process of creating, the world's most globalised higher education system, with international partnerships, faculty and qualifications, and with the English language dominating almost all new initiatives. Some of these developments, as we have noted, have been in direct response to economic demand, while others are a more general reaction to population increase and perceived learning needs. This has come at a time when international education, particularly in North America, the UK and other English-speaking countries, has become much more business oriented: foreign providers consider the business needs of their own institutions in developing international links and partnerships. On the one hand, the GCC countries have become a priority area in this market place, which may offer GCC institutions more scope themselves to develop a global reach. Their existing international partnerships can offer a basis for this. On the other hand, the pressures of this market may require education planners to look carefully at the way in which domestic development needs are being met. To what extent will the Gulf always require outside providers in this field, and does this matter?

A further issue to consider is the impact on Gulf societies of a higher education system that is largely built upon standards, systems and faculty imported from Western Europe and North America and which operates almost entirely in English. Will this style of education produce Gulf national graduates whose ideas about political and social development will reinforce rather than challenge the status quo? Should new educational undertakings also cater for the expatriate populations of the region? And is it time to consider reconnecting with some of the Arab countries that originally provided so much of the GCC's educational needs?

As regards economic relevance, to what extent are education planners, or the higher education institutions themselves, taking into account the way in which the countries of the region are seeking to shift from being 'rentier' to knowledge economies? It has been argued that the region's trajectory of economic development is now following three main paths: energy (with a strong move towards developing downstream industries and greater ownership of the energy value chain), services (especially on the model developing in Dubai) and finance capital (on a model that considers the global influence exerted by the region's massive sovereign wealth funds and the ongoing focus on finance and banking). Can this shift be made without a truly international, high-quality university system and can that system be developed sufficiently rapidly to meet the requirements of these evolving economies? How much more of the financial resources of the countries involved should be focused on higher education as part of this process?

It should not be surprising that a debate about higher education will always throw up more questions than it answers. Hopefully this volume will encourage a greater focus on the vital role that higher education has to play in the region, will close the gap in information available from the region on current educational provision and development and stimulate an open discussion of the issues and opportunities of the unique international experiment in higher education which the GCC countries are now undertaking.

ONE

Higher Education in the Gulf:
a historical background

Christopher Davidson

At the turn of the twentieth century, most visitors to the Arabian
Gulf believed socio-economic development to be non-existent in the
region, especially with regard to the advancement of formal education.
Certainly, with the hinterland of Arabia remaining isolated from
external influences and the forces of modernisation given the powerful
yet introverted Saudi–Wahhabi religious alliance,[1] and with Britain
viewing her collection of protected coastal shaikhdoms as being little
more than an informal part of her empire[2] and therefore unworthy
of receiving imperial resources for the purposes of domestic development, there was much validity to this claim, with most education
remaining informal and firmly within the bailiwick of the religious
communities. However, even without British support, between the
1920s and the 1960s a large number of new schools were established in
many of the coastal towns, with both local and expatriate Arab teachers, Arab funding, imported Arab curricula and modern, secular and
vocational subjects being taught to an increasing number of boys and
girls. Thus, while most assume that meaningful educational progress
did not really take place until after Britain's departure in 1971, after
the simultaneous creation of ministries for education in the newly

independent states, and following the massive oil-financed investments in educational infrastructure of subsequent years, there had
in effect already been an important, if sporadic, series of indigenous
or at least semi-indigenous developments.

To explain better the trajectory of this early educational progress,
it is necessary to assess the region's traditional social, economic and
political structures. In particular, I will consider the limitations of the
domestic economy and its restraints on education, the pearling boom
and the rapid development of local schools fuelled by injections of
merchant wealth, the almost equally hurried decline of these schools
following the collapse of the pearling industry, the resistance of native
merchants to dependency on Britain and their attempts to kick-start
self-directed development while concurrently reorganising the local
education system and the somewhat problematic era of assistance
from the Arab republics and Kuwait to the other Gulf shaikhdoms
in the years preceding British withdrawal. Finally, I will turn to the
original development plans drawn up by modernising monarchs in
late 1971. These aimed to reduce any future reliance on hydrocarbon
exports and to lessen the Gulf's dependency on foreign skills by
fostering a more varied economic base supported not only by superior
transport, communications and better healthcare provision, but
also by implementing a labour nationalisation programme backed
by greatly improved secondary education and the introduction of
vocational education.

1820s to 1920s – From Traditional Economy to Boom Time: the first formal schools

The Gulf was home to a number of diverse economic activities during
the nineteenth century, including fishing, animal husbandry, re-export
trading and some limited agriculture. Significantly, these were primarily at the subsistence level with rarely sufficient surplus to allow for
any meaningful growth or development.[3] As such, without necessary
resources for the building of schools or the recruitment of professional
teachers, for much of this early era the education system remained

somewhat basic. The primary form of tuition was often that provided to young men and boys by the local *mutawa'a*: ostensibly a religious man who was usually the *imam* (cleric) of the local mosque. Referred to as *al-katatib* education, this traditional *mutawa'a* system relied heavily on the rote learning of large sections of the *Qur'an* and the Prophet Muhammad's various utterances or *Hadith*. Significantly, the *mutawa'a* was rarely a literate scholar,[4] was often not the man responsible for composing the Friday prayer speeches (*al-khutbat*), and was therefore extremely unlikely to be able to teach any of the boys how to write or to comprehend rudimentary mathematics. However, for those few who did seek more knowledge, access to an educated scholar was a possibility, provided they proved their worth. Certainly, there is considerable evidence of more advanced Islamic legal education (*fiqh*) throughout this period, in addition to small 'scientific circles' that were usually held in one corner of the mosque, in a shaikh's house, or even in a tradesman's house, a prominent example being the circle of the scientists of Najd that took place in 1820 in Ra's al-Khaimah, one of Britain's protected shaikhdoms in the lower Gulf.[5]

Towards the end of the nineteenth century the region's pearling industry and its associated trades (including boat building and rope manufacturing) began to expand rapidly with profound socio-economic consequences. The shallowness of the seas combined with an abundance of the largest pearls in the world enabled local merchants alongside foreign entrepreneurs to meet massive demand for such luxuries in Bombay, Victorian Britain and other wealthy markets. Indeed, the author of Britain's *Gazetteer of the Persian Gulf, Oman and Central Asia*, John Lorimer, sought to illustrate the scale of this boom. Using estimates based on conversations with members of the merchant communities and on trade receipts, he recorded that Bahrain, Qatar and the shaikhdoms of the lower Gulf were exporting over ten *lakhs*[6] per year in the 1870s, before reaching an enormous 100 *lakhs* or one *crore* per year by the late 1890s.[7] Crucially, the region was not only enjoying an unprecedented influx of wealth during this boom, but was also beginning to experience changes in its previously simplistic economic structures. Certainly, at around the time of Lorimer's recorded pearling zenith, the industry was beginning to exhibit signs of indigenous capitalist development, with a clearly identifiable 'pearling proletariat', the *ghasa*, beginning to emerge underneath something of a capitalist class.[8]

With such newfound entrepreneurial potential, many of the Gulf's merchant families who were able to own and outfit the larger pearling boats began to grow in wealth. Prominent figures in this emerging group included Khalaf al-Otaibi and Hamid bin Buti of Abu Dhabi, Salim bin Musabbah of Dubai and Humayd bin Kamil of Sharjah.[9] Over the years, many of these prosperous notables came to exercise great political power behind the scenes, and in the case of Sharjah they were even able to replace one ruler with another as they saw fit.[10] Indeed, given that their capitalist ventures were frequently more lucrative than the rulers' more limited sources of income, it was often they who were the main financiers of any local projects, or in fact any local wars.[11] These favourable conditions were also able to attract foreign merchants, including Persians, Indians and other Arabs, all of whom brought with them fresh skills and the desire to develop their new homes in the Gulf. As such, people were optimistic: it seemed that new local activities would enjoy investment, physical infrastructure would improve, and socio-economic infrastructure would surely advance.

Certainly, with regard to education, the region's philanthropists finally had sufficient income and energy to devote to the establishment of more formal schools. Indeed, during the early part of the twentieth century, many wealthy patrons managed to found schools for boys in the Gulf. Most of these new schools were accommodated in large donated houses or in custom-made buildings, and were staffed by local men who had been educated elsewhere in the Arab world, while others were supervised by various Arab expatriates, including Egyptians and Palestinians. A much wider range of subjects was taught than ever before, often following an Egyptian curriculum. These included simple mathematics, regional geography and some Arab and European history. Examples of these early institutions would include the Al-Ahmadiya School (1912), the Al-Salmya School (1923) and the Al-Falah School (1926), all in Dubai, and the Al-Qasimi School (1923) and Al-Tatweerya (or Evolutionary) School (1907) in Sharjah. Some of the oldest Gulf nationals still alive were educated under this system, including most of the first generation of post-British Gulf rulers.[12]

1930s – Recession and the Collapse of the Education System

Despite such promising prospects for a significant expansion in education and other aspects of socio-economic development, the pearling-powered growth spurt of the Gulf's coastal towns was always destined to remain capped. Indeed, ever since the British had crossed swords with the shaikhdoms of Sharjah and Ra's al-Khaimah in the 1820s, and in 1853, in an effort to protect British–Indian trade routes, had obliged all the local rulers, including those of Kuwait, Bahrain, Qatar, Abu Dhabi and Dubai, to sign a number of self-enforcing truces (in which the rulers would agree not to attack English East India Company ships in exchange for British protection against their tribal rivals), these 'Trucial States' had gradually been drawn deeper into a network of British dependency. One of the problems for local merchants was that the truces and their associated 'exclusivity agreements' forbade them from establishing bilateral ties with other merchants outside of the British–Indian network, thereby severely inhibiting international access to markets. Furthermore, these agreements also prevented the merchants from utilising foreign technologies that would have undoubtedly led to increased growth in the pearling industry and would perhaps have even allowed for some degree of future proofing for the activity.[13] Indeed, as a descendant of one of the great pearling dynasties describes, following Britain's limiting of the size of pearling boats to carry just six or seven men (ostensibly for security reasons, but more likely to reduce any Arab competition to Britain's trade networks), as the nineteenth century progressed Britain also felt compelled to block relatively advanced pearling techniques (relating to bleaching and drilling) already being employed in the Mediterranean and the Far East from being introduced to the Gulf, 'partly because they wanted the industry to remain in Arab hands, and partly from self-interest'.[14]

Essentially, faced with increasing interference from France and other European powers in its Near Eastern spheres of influence, Britain had succeeded in transforming the Gulf into a 'British lake' sealed off from foreign interference.[15] Certainly, in Bombay it was believed that if foreign agents or merchants were ever allowed to visit and gain influence with the local rulers, then the British would stand to lose some or all of the control they had carefully established over the region earlier in the century. Britain's self-enforcing maritime treaties would be undone and its crucial trade routes to India and the Far East would once again face competition and possible security threats. Thus, by the 1930s, when the pearling industry did finally collapse, little meaningful diversification had taken place, and certainly Britain had laid no groundwork for future regional development and had provided no contingency plans. In effect, the exclusivity of markets combined with technological backwardness had rendered pearling operations in the Gulf vulnerable to advancements elsewhere, especially in Japan, where the farming of 'cultured pearls' was driving down international prices and producing larger and more attractive specimens.[16] To make matters worse, this Japanese competition came at the same time as worldwide economic depression was spreading from the core economies of the United States and the European empires. Despite its vast global reach, Britain was also suffering, and with this recession the demand for luxury items such as Gulf pearls rapidly dried up.

With most of the great powers and their colonies beginning to focus on self-survival in the build-up to the Second World War, the markets remained closed and the pearling industry never recovered. Thus, the permanence of the decline rendered the Gulf shaikhdoms poverty stricken right up until the first oil exports of the 1960s. In particular, there is little doubt that the towns of the lower Gulf were left to decay as some of Britain's poorest and least developed protectorates.

Inevitably, this ensuing poverty had major ramifications for the region's social structure, as most of the more able foreigners began to drift away, leaving something of a void in the local community. Notably, many of the activities formerly underwritten by local pearling merchants and run by Arab expatriates began to peter out, including, most conspicuously, the running of the schools. Certainly, salaries for local and other Arab teachers could not be paid, nor could the maintenance be kept up of the several schools that had been built. While there is some evidence that a few of the schools did manage to maintain a skeleton staff during the 1930s and 1940s, the consensus of this generation of schoolchildren is that there was an appreciable decline in the region's formal education, with many boys either returning to *mutawaʾa* teaching or simply not being schooled at all.[17]

1930s and 1940s – Case Study: the Dubai Education Department

By the late 1930s, a number of merchants across the Gulf were openly beginning to oppose their rulers, who were becoming increasingly regarded as British clients, thereby adding to the dependency situation of the shaikhdoms, and ultimately reducing the likelihood of autonomous economic revival and any escape from ongoing poverty. The problem was being compounded by Britain's provision of external sources of wealth for the rulers: in return for building air bases and exploring for oil, Britain was paying rent directly to the ruling families, thereby reinforcing their loyalty and elevating them above their previously prosperous domestic merchant community.[18]

In 1938 anti-British demonstrations took place in Kuwait and riots broke out in Bahrain,[19] but perhaps the strongest example of resistance occurred in Dubai when, later that year, around 400 prominent merchants[20] tried to reverse their decline and marginalisation following the collapse of the pearling industry by attempting to revitalise the lower Gulf's economy. They sought to impose reforms on their ruler, Shaikh Said bin Maktum Al Maktum, and to establish trade links outside the British-controlled networks. Led by the Al

Ghurair family and supported by the renegade Shaikh Mani bin Rashid Al Maktum and the ruler's exiled cousin, Essa bin Huraiz,[21] these men were emboldened by the unrest elsewhere in the Gulf, and a request was made to Shaikh Said to share his wealth and to allow much more of it to be managed by the community in the interests of improving domestic conditions.[22] Unlike most other rulership contests, Dubai's merchants did not therefore actively seek to depose their ruler. Instead these reformers together with other disgruntled notables set up a new consultative *majlis* (meeting room) in which the ruler would be recognised as the president of a fifteen-member chamber, but in exchange would have to share seven-eighths of Dubai's total revenue.[23] The shared revenue was to be spent in the name of the state and only with the prior approval of the members of the new *majlis*.

Although this merchants' *majlis* operated for only a brief period, the correspondence and minutes of their meetings make it clear that its members intended to bring about key changes in the socio-economic infrastructure.[24] Indeed, the *majlis* quickly established a number of important institutions including a municipal council, in addition to planning for a social security system for the elderly, and electing new civil servants to be employed by the state, not the ruler.[25] Most significantly, the movement also made a considerable financial contribution to Dubai's education system and made concerted efforts to re-open Dubai's schools. Indeed, the *majlis* established the first proper education department, appointed a Director General for Dubai schools, and even managed to recruit the majority of teachers from the local population (many of whom were older Dubai men who had been educated when schools had flourished during the pearling boom).[26]

Unfortunately, although the reformers enjoyed much popular support for their actions, their movement and its products, including the new municipality and the education department, were ultimately short lived. By emasculating their ruler they had considerably weakened a client of the British and were operating outside the Imperial zone of control. Thus, when in 1939 the merchants' *majlis* attempted to add even more limitations to the ruler's income by allowing him to retain just 10,000 rupees of the state's revenue for 'personal use', Shaikh Said was forced to resort to military means.[27] Following the dispersal of the merchants and the breaking-up of the *majlis*, British aircraft flew over Dubai at low altitude while dropping leaflets in defence of the ruler that erroneously claimed the merchants' movement had collapsed due to mismanagement and a lack of popular support.[28]

1950s and 1960s – Continuing Poverty and Kuwaiti Assistance for Education

Despite the collapse of the reform movement and the immediate unravelling of all of its hard work, it must be noted how many of its actions and suggestions were not without some long-term achievement, with many of them forming the blueprints for later initiatives across the Gulf that were often undertaken by the rulers themselves. Notably, in the 1950s Shaikh Said and his new ruling council attempted to rejuvenate many of the merchants' planned improvements in an effort to boost Dubai's commercial prosperity.[29] Furthermore, upon his succession in 1958, one of Shaikh Rashid bin Said Al Maktum's very first acts was to re-establish the Dubai Municipal Council and the Education Department, despite championing his father's cause against it just twenty years previously. The Municipal Council, when founded, appointed councillors to represent different sections of the community for periods of two years. It was empowered to make the necessary orders for the administration of the town and to administer Dubai's first official development plans, all of which were commissioned by the ruler and prepared by British experts.[30]

Even with a reinstated municipality and education department, the problem of poverty and lack of resources still remained, and Britain remained largely uninterested in investing in schools, hospitals or other aspects of social infrastructure. However, by this stage some areas of the Gulf, notably Kuwait, were becoming increasingly prosperous, as they were already beginning to receive sizeable revenues from their oil exports, and by the early 1960s the poorer parts of the Gulf were beginning to receive considerable financial assistance in rebuilding their society. Although the exact motivations of the greatest benefactor, Kuwait's Shaikh Abdullah Salem Al Sabah,[31] remain unclear (it is possible that the Kuwaiti monarchy, supported by Britain, wished to improve education elsewhere in the Gulf to help prevent the spread of Arab nationalism and other revolutionary sentiments),[32] there is little doubt that Kuwaiti aid was a key catalyst for the development of education across the region.

Most of this aid was channelled through Kuwait's Gulf Permanent Assistance Committee (GUPAC). The committee's primary task was to finance the salaries of the expatriate teachers (who were again predominantly Egyptian and Palestinian), while also helping to train more local teachers, construct more schools and establish an overseas scholarship system for talented young men[33] (most of whom were able to study in Egypt and Syria).[34] Indeed, Kuwaiti generosity even extended to paying for Western-style school uniforms and shoes,[35] and invariably provided school stationery complete with the embossed emblem of the Kuwaiti government. The number of subjects taught in the schools was again expanded, this time to include English, more international history and some basic natural science. Almost all teachers followed the Kuwaiti curriculum (except the science classes),[36] which at that time was widely regarded as one of the most progressive in the Arab world, and was of course culturally more acceptable and appropriate than the previously used Egyptian curriculum. Organised around two academic semesters, these schools had relatively strict requirements for their pupils, and at the end of each year issued certificates that were necessary for children to advance to a higher level. There were around eight such levels or grades, and class sizes (usually around thirty to forty pupils) would therefore consist of a variety of ages from five years old to sixteen, depending on individual levels of progress.[37]

The most notable examples of improved schools would include the aforementioned Al-Ahmadiya School in Dubai that had massively expanded to around 820 students in 1951 and the original Al-Qasimi School in Sharjah, which benefited from major expansion in 1954.

New schools included those at Al-Falahiya and Al-Batin in Abu Dhabi, which both began to accommodate around 115 students by 1961, and another school in Abu Dhabi's second city of Al-'Ayn which housed around seventy students. Importantly, Kuwaiti aid also catalysed female education and other more specialised forms of training in the lower Gulf by providing the bulk of the funding for the new Khawla bint al-Azwar School in Dubai for girls, by opening a small number of trade and technical schools in Sharjah and Dubai, by supplying funds for an agricultural school in Ra's al-Khaimah,[38] and by opening Bahrain's first school for adult illiterates in 1968.[39]

Although not on the same scale as Kuwaiti assistance, it is also significant that other countries began to respond to Shaikh Abdullah's initiative and also sought to build up the Gulf's education system. While the political motivations behind such moves were again ambiguous, with regard to improving education the results were nevertheless impressive. In parallel to building his (now iconic) hospital in Dubai, the Shah of Iran established an Iranian school to provide education for the large number of children belonging to the city's well-established Iranian merchant community. Similarly generous, the university-educated Shaikh Muhammad bin Saud of Saudi Arabia established specific Islamic education institutions in Dubai (1962), Bahrain (1963), Al-'Ayn (1967), Ra's al-Khaimah (1967) and 'Ajman (1969). Servicing the Gulf's huge Indian resident population, after 1966 a number of wealthy Indians invested in local education by importing teachers from Bombay and establishing schools, many of which continue to exist today and have since expanded to include several sister schools.[40]

Notwithstanding the rapid progress of formal education during this period, there were complications associated with the foreign aid, the influx of new teachers and the use of foreign curricula. Most notably in Abu Dhabi, Shaikh Shakhbut bin Sultan Al Nahayan remained in power until 1966 and was largely distrustful of foreigners. This distrust manifested itself in restrictions placed on all merchants, bans on new construction[41] and, on occasion, blocks on the usage of

Kuwaiti textbooks in Abu Dhabi's schools. Indeed, it is reported that in 1956 Shaikh Shakhbut set up another new school in Abu Dhabi, but given that he wanted the school to be 'concerned with the affairs of Abu Dhabi alone', he did not permit any foreign teachers to work in it.[42] Also problematic was the issue of Arab nationalism which, during the 1950s and 1960s, was running rife throughout the Arab world following the demise of British-backed monarchs in Egypt, Syria, Iraq and eventually Libya. Given that many of the Kuwaiti-financed teachers who were brought in to staff the new schools in the Gulf were often nationals of these revolutionary states or at least sympathetic to their cause, there was a genuine concern from both the Gulf's ruling families and British administrators that this reliance on Arab expatriate educational assistance could backfire, causing instability and turmoil.

Such worries were not without foundation, with many of the Arab nationalist activities that took place in the region being directly linked to school teachers and clubs of impressionable students. Perhaps the first example of organised secular nationalism in the region was when a group was set up in the early 1950s in Dubai's Al-Falah School. Many of the Iraqi teachers there had begun to spread their nationalist sentiments and, as eyewitnesses described, they encouraged many of their pupils to 'parade through the narrow streets of the town, carrying flags and chanting Arab nationalist songs, applauded by their parents and citizens'.[43] Similarly, at the time of the Suez Crisis there were again demonstrations, this time by a number of teachers and local youths wishing to express their sympathy with Egypt in the fight against Israeli invasion and what was perceived to be an anti-Arab, Anglo-French collaboration.[44] Moreover, it is possible that some of these chose to join the Front for the Liberation of Occupied Eastern Arabia (FLOEA), an underground nationalist group which advocated violent action to 'end British colonialism and overthrow the ruling oligarchy'.[45] Indeed, a group of students was caught trying to set fire to the British air base in Sharjah as an act of protest,[46] and these may well have been FLOEA members. Later, during the final year of the short-lived United Arab Republic in 1961, tensions again flared as a result of expatriate teachers: many of the young boys in the Gulf's schools were encouraged by the senior students and the Egyptian, Syrian and Iraqi members of staff to mount large-scale demonstrations down the streets while carrying banners and photos of Jamal Abdul Nasser, the Egyptian president.[47]

1970s – New Priorities and the First Ministries for Education

Following Britain's elegiac withdrawal from the Gulf in 1971, there were clearly fresh priorities for the education systems in the newly independent Bahrain and Qatar, and in the newly created United Arab Emirates. First, given the ongoing reliance on foreign aid and its associated complications, a much larger homegrown cadre of educated schoolteachers was required. Furthermore, on a more macro level, the citizens of these nascent 'emirates' needed to be rapidly trained to fill a wide range of public and private sector positions that were being created by the concurrent oil boom. If this was not done then almost all key administrative positions would end up being occupied by expatriates. As such, in the early 1970s, higher-quality education had already been identified as a building block for any future labour nationalisation process. Indeed, it was recognised that the initial employment system of imposing quotas and other more punitive measures on companies employing too many foreigners would eventually need to be replaced by an educational system that produced genuinely well-schooled and competitive local labour.[48]

The first steps were the creation of ministries for education that would have adequate funding to assume responsibility for the existing 'state' schools, thereby ending the bulk of foreign educational aid. One of the initial problems these ministries faced was the accommodation of the large number of children who were still outside the formal schooling system. Indeed, despite the years of Kuwaiti assistance that had seen the number of enrolled students in the Gulf increase from around 4,000 to 28,000, this was still only a fraction of the total youth population. Moreover, the bulk of these students were males, as the number of school places for girls remained very low. Furthermore, literacy rates for the over-sixteen-year-olds were still below 50 per cent for males and 30 per cent for females in 1971.[49]

The solution was to increase rapidly the number of schools and to expand further the existing ones. In the UAE's case, following a major construction drive, the federal ministry for education succeeded in raising the number of state schools from 129 in 1972 to 383 by the end of the decade. An increased proportion of the schools was for girls, and the number of students increased threefold while the number of teachers (including a greater number of local instructors) quadrupled, thereby improving the staff–student ratios. For the first time, kindergarten schools were introduced (for those aged four to five), while the years of primary education were more clearly defined (with grades one to six), and followed by separate middle (grades seven to nine) and secondary schools (grades ten and above).[50]

With regard to the curricula used by these new schools, the new ministries did not have the time or resources to develop locally specific textbooks, given the number of other, more pressing tasks their employees were currently faced with. Therefore, the old Kuwaiti curriculum remained in place a little longer, allowing the Gulf's schools to consolidate the subjects that were first introduced in the 1950s and 1960s. However, as the ministries took charge of the trade and technical schools, and added new ones, they were required to act much faster, creating new syllabuses geared to training their youth in up-to-date engineering techniques and all of the other vocational studies prioritised by the labour nationalisation strategies. Indeed, as Gulf nationals educated during the early 1970s recall, they faced a curious mixture of textbooks throughout their school career: books used during primary and middle schools regularly featured examples and illustrations (sometimes obscure) relating to Kuwait or other parts of the Arab world, with pictures of often unfamiliar shaikhs, emirs or presidents on the front inset pages, while those who later began to train for employment in the oil companies or in the manufacturing sector were provided with material clearly written in their home country, with prominent pictures of their rulers displayed throughout.

Conclusion

A native, or rather a hybrid native and expatriate, Arab educational system had emerged in the Gulf's coastal shaikhdoms by the time of British withdrawal. Given the relative poverty of the region before the onset of oil revenues it is perhaps little surprise that the main proponents and financiers of education were not rulers or governments, but were instead wealthy pearling merchants or representatives of more prosperous Arab states. Many of these reformers were already locked in a struggle with Britain as they attempted to free themselves of dependent economic relations, and given that many of the main suppliers of schoolteachers were Arab nationalist republics, it is understandable how closely intertwined the region's educational development became with British and pan-Arab politics. Nevertheless, despite such complications, the poorer parts of the Gulf were still able to inherit at least some educational infrastructure in 1971, and were by no means starting from scratch.

In particular, although erratic, the long history of educational development had allowed for the gradual secularisation of education in most of the Gulf. This process had begun early in the twentieth century with the establishment of non-religious schools, and by the late 1960s the process was more or less complete, with the vast majority of those receiving education being taught by staff employed by schools, not solely by members of the religious community. In turn, by 1971 this secularisation aided the new ministries' task of offering more vocational courses aimed at facilitating labour nationalisation; with religious education as a mere component of a broader national curriculum, their administrators could press ahead with developing modern, technical courses, without fearing any conservative opposition.

Similarly, this long and gradual process also helped to improve access to education for all sections of the population and, in some cases, reduced previous social inequalities. Most obviously, as described, there were specific schools for girls. These schools revolutionised female education in the Gulf and considerably improved the socio-economic opportunities for young women in what had previously been a restricted, patriarchal society in which only boys could hope to receive formal education. Crucially, many of the women educated by these schools were the mothers and grandmothers of the present generation of Gulf national females, most of whom are now expected by their respective governments and ruling families to be well educated, open-minded, competitive and willing to enter the labour force. Moreover, the opportunities provided by these early schools allowed for young men from less privileged sections of the population, especially the recently urbanised *bedu*, to improve their situations. Although tribal politics have always been present in the region, and in some cases continue to create glass ceilings of employment for certain tribes and families in the Gulf today, there is little doubt that during this period if one performed well at school, the chances of gaining an overseas scholarship were increased, and if one returned to the region after receiving such an education, the chances of gaining a key position of responsibility were high, given the relatively small number of educated men at that time.

Notes

1. See Donald Hawley, *The Trucial States*, London 1970, p. 101.
2. For a greater discussion of Britain's informal empire in the Gulf, see James Onley, *The Arabian Frontier of the British Raj: merchants, rulers, and the British in the nineteenth century Gulf*, Oxford 2007.
3. Hawley, p. 195.
4. A scholar was sometimes referred to as *al-shaikh*, but for the purposes of this discussion this term would cause confusion with the title given to the ruler of a tribe.
5. Personal interviews with members of the Al Omram, Al Mazroui, Al Marzouqi and Al Qasimi families, Dubai, May 2006.
6. A *lakh* being 100,000 rupees.
7. John Lorimer, *Gazetteer of the Persian Gulf, Oman and Central Arabia*, Calcutta 1970, p. 2252.
8. Ibid., p. 2228. A great deal of information about the pearling proletariat and their treatment by captains and financiers is contained in the interviews recorded in Abdullah Abd al-Rahman's substantive work, *The Emirates in*

the Memory of its Children, Dubai 1990, pp. 90–1 (in Arabic).

9.   For a list of other prominent merchant families see Muhammad A. Mutawwa, *Development and Social Change in the Emirates*, Beirut 1991, p. 31 (in Arabic).

10. Muhammad Morsy Abdullah, *The United Arab Emirates: a modern history*, London 1978, p. 104.

11. Muhammad G. Al-Rumaithi, 'The Mode of Production in the Arab Gulf before the Discovery of Oil', in Tim Niblock, ed., *Social and Economic Development in the Arab Gulf*, London 1980, p. 49.

12. Personal interviews with members of the Al Omram and Al Marzouqi families, Dubai, May 2006.

13. Christopher M. Davidson, *The United Arab Emirates: a study in survival*, Boulder 2005, pp. 29–34.

14. Muhammad Al-Fahim, *From Rags to Riches: a story of Abu Dhabi*, London 1995, pp. 22–4.

15. David Roberts, 'The Consequences of the Exclusive Treaties: a British view' in B. Pridham, ed., *The Arab Gulf and the West*, London 1985.

16. See Kevin Fenelon, *The United Arab Emirates: an economic and social survey*, London 1973, p. 56; and Hawley, p. 197.

17. Personal interviews with members of the Al Mazroui family, Dubai, May 2006.

18. Davidson, pp. 34–7.

19. Jacqueline S. Ismael, *Kuwait: dependency and class in a rentier state*, Gainesville 1993, pp. 152–3; and Frauke Heard-Bey, *From Trucial States to United Arab Emirates*, London 1996, p. 255.

20. Hendrik Van Der Meulen, 'The Role of Tribal and Kinship Ties in the Politics of the United Arab Emirates', PhD Dissertation, Fletcher School of Law and Diplomacy 1997, p. 338.

21. Personal interviews, Dubai, May 2005 and February 2006.

22. Abdullah, p. 126.

23. 'Total revenue' included all income derived from oil concessions and air agreements: see Albadr Abu Baker, 'Political Economy of State Formation: the United Arab Emirates in comparative perspective', PhD Dissertation, University of Michigan 1995, p. 107.

24. Heard-Bey, p. 256.

25. Abdullah, p. 131.

26. Ibid., p. 109.

27. Shaikh Said regained control over all of Dubai after unleashing a loyal contingent of *bedu*. See Heard-Bey, p. 256.

28. Abdullah, pp. 132–3.

29. Fatma Al-Sayegh, 'Merchants' Role in a Changing Society: the case of Dubai, 1900–1990', in *Middle Eastern Studies*, vol. 34, no. 1, 1996.

30. Abdullah, pp. 134–6. The first development plan was commissioned in

1960.

31. Personal interviews with members of the Al Omram family, Dubai, May 2006.

32. Muhammad Salih al-Musfir, 'The United Arab Emirates: an assessment of federalism in a developing polity', PhD Dissertation, State University of New York at Binghamton 1985, pp. 92–3.

33. Fenelon, pp. 26–7; al-Musfir, pp. 92–3.

34. PRO (Public Records Office, London) 371/120540, 1956.

35. PRO 371/120540, 1956.

36. According to oral history accounts, the science classes remained with the Egyptian curriculum throughout the 1960s. Proxy interview with Farida al-Madani, Dubai, February 2006.

37. Proxy interview with Nasser Ali al-Madani, Dubai, February 2006.

38. PRO 371/120553, 1956.

39. Personal interviews with members of the Al Marzouqi family, Dubai, May 2006.

40. Personal interviews with members of the Al Qasimi and Al Marzouqi families, Dubai, May 2006.

41. Davidson, pp. 156–7.

42. PRO 371/120553, 1956.

43. Abdullah, p. 112.

44. Ibid., p. 74.

45. Najat Abdullah Al-Nabeh, 'The United Arab Emirates: regional and global dimensions', PhD Dissertation, Claremont Graduate School 1984, pp. 121–3. Al-Nabeh contends that this group had close ties with the Dhufar Liberation Front in Oman.

46. Abdullah, p. 144.

47. Personal interviews with members of the Al Qasimi family, Dubai, May 2006.

48. Davidson, pp. 150–4.

49. Personal interviews with members of the Al Omram family, Dubai, May 2006.

50. Personal interviews with members of the Al Mazroui family, Dubai, May 2006.

TWO

Reforming Higher Education : the GCC highway in the shadow of the World Bank road

Mari Luomi

The expectations facing national higher education systems are increasingly global. Universities are required to produce the right mix of high-skilled, competitive and innovative graduates, alongside conducting meaningful research; governments are expected to invest increasingly in research and development; the importance of a functioning and balanced relationship between the supply of the academically educated and the corresponding demand in the market is recognised in both the developed and developing world while concepts such as gender equality, relevance, quality, access, equal opportunities and lifelong learning are now almost universal aims for all states that strive to become high-performing knowledge economies. These challenges are difficult to manage for even the most competitive of economies, but they are particularly so for those developing countries that traditionally have had little experience of higher education and now find themselves facing the same expectations as countries that have had centuries of experience in the field. The six Gulf monarchies, which established their first institutions of higher education between the 1950s and 1970s, are a good example of this.

Over the last decade, these and other issues relating to higher education reforms in developing countries have been addressed in a variety of contexts at both international and regional levels in such international organisations as UNESCO,[1] the United Nations Development Program (UNDP),[2] the Organisation for Economic Cooperation and Development (OECD), the World Economic Forum[3] and the World Bank. The 1998 UNESCO *World Declaration on Higher Education* adopted human rights as the starting-point of its framework for renewal of higher education in the twenty-first century. It recalled the principles of economic, social, cultural, civil and political rights and then proceeded to address issues of equity, access to education, participation, quality, relevance and diversification, while stressing the importance of international cooperation in converting the 'brain drain' from developing economies into a 'brain gain' for these societies.[4] The UNDP's *Arab Human Development Report* of 2003 concentrated on the role of knowledge in development. The vision outlined in the report included five pillars: transparency of educational structures, quality of education, science and research, knowledge-based production and the development of an Arab knowledge model. Most importantly, it emphasised that structural obstacles to fulfil these aims were social, economic and, most importantly, political.[5]

In 2008 the World Bank issued a report entitled *The Road Not Traveled: education reform in the Middle East and North Africa*, that shared similar ideas with these previous documents on the desired goals of higher education but examined the topic from a very different angle. As a lending institution the primary interest of the World Bank is understandably related to economic growth and functional markets, and this consequently affects the approach applied by its analysts to educational reforms. *The Road Not Traveled*, an extensive study written by a team of twenty-two economists and other experts, has the economic returns of investments in education of the countries in the Middle East and North Africa (MENA) as its main concern.

The report argues that the MENA countries need to develop a new approach to educational reform as well as pay more attention to the relationship between labour markets and education. In order to achieve better effectiveness and competitiveness these countries should move from 'command and control' structures towards 'coordination and evaluation' and increase accountability to the public. However, it is also vital that the supply and demand of educated individuals are balanced so that the educational reforms can have the optimal effect.[6]

Despite recognising the heterogeneity of the countries in the Middle East and Northern Africa, the World Bank report describes the region with a markedly homogenising approach and, consequently, suggests a largely uniform policy prescription for this 'imagined community' of around twenty states. Yet, during the last decade, since the 1998 UNESCO declaration, the GCC states have taken enormous steps in reforming their educational systems and are currently far ahead of most states in the Mashriq and Maghrib regions in terms of both intensity and pace. The almost chronic assimilatory approach of international organisations to the 'Arab world plus Iran' is problematic because it inhibits the perception of the differentiated dynamics currently affecting educational systems in the three aforementioned sub-regions, especially in the case of the GCC. The recent developments in the field of higher education in the GCC countries are particularly illustrative of this problem and will hence be the focus of this chapter.

For the purposes of a sub-region and sector specific contemplation, this chapter will examine the World Bank report *The Road Not Traveled* by asking the following questions: does the regional, multi-level perspective on education reforms in the World Bank report allow for sufficient consideration of the special characteristics of sub-regional groups of countries in the tertiary sector of education? In other words, does the analysis in the report adequately take note of the similarities and differences in the current state of higher education in the Gulf monarchies, either as a bloc or as individual states, with relation to the rest of the MENA region?

In order to answer the questions, the chapter will focus on the main findings and policy recommendations of *The Road Not Traveled* with a sub-regional focus on the GCC states and a sectoral focus on tertiary education and its relationship with the labour markets in the region. First, the chapter will give a brief overview of the structure of the World Bank report and discuss the main problems of the research design of the report with relation to the special focus areas. Second, the text will examine more closely some of the main findings of the report in relation to the six GCC countries and see how the report accounts for the changes that have taken place during the last decade in the area of higher education in these states. Finally, the chapter will draw a conclusion on whether the World Bank report is successful in accounting for the developments in tertiary education in the Gulf monarchies.

Main Findings of *The Road Not Traveled*

In its analysis, *The Road Not Traveled* takes a comprehensive approach to educational reform. The decision to include all levels of instruction stems, according to the authors, from the overarching nature of the problems each national educational system faces and the fact that human capital and economic growth are closely linked.[7] The report consists of an extensive analysis of both quantitative and qualitative material from the period of 1970 to 2003, in altogether 360 pages, including short case studies and a statistical appendix. The authors state clearly that their main focus is on the economic rather than the socio-cultural dimension of education and that the purpose of the publication is to equip policymakers in the region with tools for drafting new policies and strategies. The study encompasses most of the Arab League states and Iran – although a telling detail is that the authors do not specify which countries are included in the term MENA.[8] In essence, the report examines the socio-economic returns created by past investments in education in the MENA region and compares these outcomes both intraregionally and with other developing regions, namely Latin America and East Asia (chapters 1–3). It also assesses country-specific reform strategies by using a framework developed by the authors of the report in order to find out which kind of approaches to educational reform have produced the best results (chapters 4–6). Finally, the report examines domestic and external labour markets of countries in the MENA region and how these function in relation to the supply of an educated workforce (chapters 7–8).[9]

First, the report evaluates the impact of investments in education on economic growth, income distribution and poverty alleviation The conclusion from the first chapters is that much has been achieved in a short time but not enough: the MENA countries are not effective or competitive enough internationally. According to the report, investment in human capital as such does not necessarily produce economic development and, therefore, other growth-enhancing policies are also needed.[10] In the second part, the authors develop a framework for educational reform by proposing a mix of three different perspectives: one that emphasises technical issues, mainly management and funding of the system, another that concentrates on the principal–agent (policymakers–schools/ teachers) relationship and incentives, and a third that stresses public accountability and mechanisms of bottom-up influence on the system. By analysing a sample of fourteen countries – with Kuwait and Saudi Arabia as the only GCC states included – the report concludes that past reforms have concentrated too heavily on the first approach, *engineering*, and that those countries that 'give their citizens more voice broadly and education-specific voice mechanisms in particular', such as Kuwait, have better educational systems and outcomes.[11] The third part analyses domestic labour markets and migration trends in the region and observes that the demand for an educated workforce is often low because of low economic growth or is distorted because of different government policies, such as public sector employment placements, which is a major factor, especially in the oil producing countries. Migration is also handled ineffectively and unsystematically even when it is left to function according to market forces, which leads to either underemployment (that is, underutilisation of labour) or open unemployment in the MENA countries.[12]

The fact that *The Road Not Traveled* does not define what it includes in the MENA region but still gives policy recommendations that are directed to its policymakers, illustrates well some of the main problems of the research design of the report. While the authors occasionally point to the diversity of the MENA region and to the difficulty of making generalisations,[13] most of the conclusions of the report extend to the entire region, including the principal conclusion that the 'MENA (region) has yet to fully embark on the road of reforming its education systems to satisfy its development needs ... (and) has yet to catch up with the more dynamic economies of the newly industrialized world'.[14] This approach blurs the line between country-specific and general. Most importantly, by approaching the region through its similarities, the authors miss out an important point in the analysis: the Gulf monarchies have already embarked on the road of reforms and are advancing at a dizzying speed.

From the viewpoint of the tertiary sector of education in the GCC countries, the main deficiencies of the World Bank report are related to sample design and the data's insufficient inclusion in the analysis.[15] The main analysis, in chapters 5 to 6, in which the country-specific combinations of the three perspectives to educational reform are examined empirically, is based on a sample of fourteen countries. Of the total of nineteen countries covered by the report, four of the five left out of the analysis are GCC states (Bahrain, Oman, Qatar and the United Arab Emirates). Notwithstanding the stated difficulty of comparison in situations where there are no (consistent) data available for a country[16] – a partially invalid explanation for an organisation as eminent and influential as the World Bank – the report makes a mistake in extrapolating most of its conclusions to all the MENA states even when it has not studied all of them.[17]

Returns to Investment in Education –
Tertiary Education in the GCC

The first part of *The Road Not Traveled* focuses on investment in education and its socio-economic impact Regarding public expenditure on education during the period from 1995 to 2003, MENA countries spent on average 5.3 per cent of GDP on education, which was higher than in Latin America (3.9 per cent) and East Asia (3.6 per cent).[18] The GCC states present a highly uneven spending pattern, with Kuwait and Saudi Arabia spending on average 6.3 per cent, Oman and Bahrain 3.9 and 3.6 per cent respectively, and the United Arab Emirates (UAE) only 1.7 per cent of GDP on education.[19] There seems to be no correlation between the affluence of a country and its spending on education as a proportion of the GDP among the MENA countries. The report discovers that past investments, even though high, were not associated with economic growth in the region. Among the factors obstructing growth the report mentions the role of the public sector as an employer and the advantages associated with working for the government.[20]

Attendance in tertiary education in the Gulf monarchies has increased substantially from 1980, when the average gross enrolment rate was only around 6 per cent, to 2003, when the average was 23 per cent, thus increasing by almost fourfold in a little more than two decades. Throughout the period observed in the report, the GCC countries followed the MENA average of tertiary gross enrolment, which was 10 per cent in 1980 and grew to 24 per cent in 2003. However, Bahrain and Saudi Arabia stand out for their high levels of higher education enrolment, 34 and 28 per cent respectively in 2003. On the other end of the scale there is Oman with only a 13 per cent enrolment ratio in the same year. Despite remarkable development in a relatively short period of time, the GCC and MENA had not yet reached the levels of enrolment attained by East Asia (38 per cent) and Latin America (37 per cent) by 2003. This, according to the World Bank, indicates that the level of human capital in the GCC and the MENA is still quite low.[21] The report, however, does not take into account the apparently unknown number of young men that leave the Gulf each year to complete their degrees abroad before returning to contribute significantly to the level of national human capital in these states.

In five of the GCC countries, excluding Kuwait, an average of 70 per cent of all university students in 2002/03 majored in education, humanities and social sciences. The equivalent average for all MENA countries was 63 per cent while those for East Asia and Latin America were 54 and 57 per cent respectively.[22] According to the authors, this pattern of enrolment of the MENA countries, which in the observed years was clearly even more pronounced in the Gulf monarchies, is 'historically consistent with a policy of absorbing most university graduates into civil service jobs, but is ill suited to a development strategy that draws on private initiatives and dynamic manufacturing and service sectors'.[23] The World Bank report concludes its observation on the quality of human capital by pointing out that 'given the very high average income per capita, the oil states, such as Bahrain, Kuwait and Saudi Arabia, all seem to provide, on average, lower quality education than most other MENA countries'.[24] According to the report, generally speaking, regional similarities in socio-economic development in the MENA include high levels of investment in education, increasing gender parity and policies of guaranteed employment in the public sector.[25]

The New Challenges and the Gulf Monarchies

The challenges the education systems of most MENA countries now face, according to *The Road Not Traveled*, are related to globalisation, the role of knowledge in development and the increasingly competitive global environment. There will also be a growing number of young people seeking secondary and higher education, which not only requires more funds but also diversification of the system in terms of providing different opportunities and efficiency in transferring skills and competencies.[26] In order to measure the level of development of a country towards the knowledge economy, the World Bank has developed the Knowledge Economy Index (KEI). In 2007, the GCC countries were ranked more highly in the index than the rest of the MENA. Qatar scored the highest, at 42nd, and Saudi Arabia the lowest, at 69th. The KEI average score for the GCC countries was 5.57, which is slightly higher than the MENA average (5.3) but is less than the world average (5.93) and still remains far from that of Western Europe (8.7). [27]

The population of the MENA region in general has increased rapidly during the past half a century and it has almost quadrupled in the countries covered by the World Bank report: from 80 million in 1950 to 310 million in 2000. Moreover, according to United Nations statistics, population in this region is expected to reach 580 million by 2025. In the Gulf monarchies the population increased over sevenfold from the 1950s, when the total population of the six countries was little over 4 million, to 2000, when it was almost 30 million. Demographic growth in the sub-region was most extensive in the 1980s when the population of the GCC states increased by 9.3 million.[28] According to the World Bank report, the pace of growth in the MENA has been higher than in any other region in the world and, on average, growth rates fell back only in the 1980s due to increased equitable access to education, especially for women. Consequently, the share of youth in the population will continue to be higher than in other regions for decades to come.[29]

Owing to high fertility rates in the past, there is currently a large cohort of young people who will increase the demand for education in the near future and raise the need for different educational outcomes. Among the GCC states, the authors estimate that increases in demand for tertiary education will peak in Kuwait and Bahrain by 2035. Saudi Arabia will experience this by 2045 whereas in Oman, Qatar and the UAE the primary education cohort will still continue to grow until 2050. The report states that, in the future, all MENA countries, the GCC included, will have to progress by a great leap in dealing with demand for secondary and tertiary education.[30]

Success of the Reforms – Higher Education in
Saudi Arabia and Kuwait

In the second part of *The Road Not Traveled* the authors develop an educational reform framework for the MENA countries and test it empirically by observing and comparing how fourteen countries, first ranked according to their performance in balancing the three approaches of engineering, incentives and public accountability in their educational systems, perform in the four variables of access, equity, quality and efficiency.[31] In this analysis only Kuwait and Saudi Arabia were included from the GCC. Regarding access to higher education, in comparison to the countries of the sample on tertiary gross enrolment rates, Kuwait and Saudi Arabia were among the middle performers with rates of 22 per cent and 28 per cent respectively in 2003. Had the report taken into account the other GCC countries in the analysis, Bahrain (34 per cent) would have ranked among the best performers, after Lebanon (48 per cent), Jordan (39 per cent) and West Bank and Gaza (38 per cent) in 2003. Oman, in turn, would have been among the low-end performers, while the enrolment rates for higher education of Qatar and the UAE were near the MENA average in 2002/03.[32]

The gender parity index of tertiary education, one of the indicators of equity, sets the GCC countries clearly apart from the rest of the MENA countries. The World Bank report does not take notice of the fact that the Gulf monarchies reached gender parity in this sector far before the rest of the countries in the region. Nevertheless, as was mentioned earlier, a large number of men in these countries earn their academic degrees abroad, thus causing a distortion in the national statistics to the benefit of women. By 1970, Bahrain had a parity index of 1.3 and Kuwait of 1.2. The first available data for Qatar (1975) indicate that there were already 3.6 females for each male enrolled and, similarly, 1.9 females for each male in the UAE (1980). Oman and Saudi Arabia had both reached gender parity in tertiary education by 2000. The Maghrib countries – except Morocco – had only attained gender parity by early 2000 and some, but not all, of the Mashriq countries in the 1990s or early 2000s. In the sample of fourteen, Kuwait also fares well according to the Gini coefficient of average years of schooling (of adults aged 15 and over), ranking among the top three, and ranks first in the 'integrated index for equity' produced for the purposes of the report. The report produces no information on the other four GCC countries so further comparisons are not possible.[33]

With regard to quality, the authors chose to use literacy rates and international test scores for mathematics and science as indicators. In the comparison between the fourteen countries, Kuwait scored high in both indicators and Saudi Arabia well in adult literacy. In levels of adult literacy the GCC countries fare better than the MENA average.[34] Nevertheless, female adult illiteracy still remains higher than male illiteracy in all GCC countries except for the UAE, where in 2003 one-quarter of the male population was illiterate compared to one-fifth of the female, a phenomenon resulting from the large number of blue-collar expatriates originating from poorer countries.[35] Efficiency, in turn, was measured in the report with primary education completion rates. In this comparison, Kuwait ranks fourth and Saudi Arabia second last, faring only better than Djibouti.[36]

In the overall comparison between the fourteen countries of the sample, Kuwait ranks second, after Jordan, whereas Saudi Arabia ranks tenth. The report concludes that the main challenges for the best-performing countries will relate to retention at higher levels of education, higher external efficiency (such as addressing human capital needs in society) and higher levels of instructional quality at all levels. Saudi Arabia is mentioned as having 'an unusual mix of relatively high rates of literacy accompanied by low levels of primary enrolment'. The quite obvious policy recommendation of the authors here is to 'consolidate past achievements and tackle whatever unique problems (the) country faces'. An important finding for the GCC is that success in meeting educational objectives does not always seem to correlate with per capita income. The diverging results between Kuwait and Jordan, on the one hand, and Saudi Arabia, on the other, are a tenable indicator of this.[37] The authors also found out that high performers of the sample, including Kuwait, have sought to widen and diversify the available funding for education by fees and private provision of education especially in higher education. In addition to a greater participation of the private sector, the report finds that these states also have better evaluation, monitoring and rewarding mechanisms in public schools. The report argues that the private sector needs to be engaged, especially in the tertiary sector, though in a balanced manner. Lastly, despite the small size of the sample, the authors argue that the results of the empirical analysis suggest that the predictions regarding the reform model hold in the region and possibly even outside it, namely, that educational systems tend to be more successful when they mix all the three elements of the World Bank framework.[38]

Labour Markets and Policy Environments

In its final section the report addresses labour markets and the related policy environment with a reminder that labour market outcomes ultimately determine economic returns from education and translate human capital into growth. According to the report, labour market outcomes are weak in most of the countries in the MENA region. They cannot respond quickly enough to accommodate the growing labour force, especially in the case of women and the (highly) educated; a great proportion of the educated therefore find themselves unemployed or in low-productivity jobs. The World Bank report states that reforms are needed in 'public sector employment policies, the private sector development agenda, and the informality of a large segment of economic activities.'[39] Some of the findings of the report related to the role of the public sector and academic unemployment in the GCC will be discussed below.

The World Bank report emphasises the fact that human capital in the public sector does not contribute to economic growth and reduces it when government workers abuse their powers and generate rent for themselves. Levels of public sector employment and, consequently, expenditure on public sector wages, in the MENA countries are still among the highest in the world. This, according to the authors, is especially true in the GCC countries where public sector investment has served as a way of distributing oil wealth. For example, in Kuwait the public sector increased its employment of nationals from 76 per cent in 1975 to 92 per cent in 1985. Even in 2000, public sector employment among the nationals in the GCC countries averaged at 70 per cent. Country-specific figures for this year were available in the report for Bahrain (28 per cent), Kuwait (93 per cent) and Saudi Arabia (79 per cent). The MENA and OECD averages for the same year were 29 per cent and 14 per cent.[40]

In GCC countries the rise of the public sector has also led to a segmentation of the labour market between nationals and expatriates. The segmentation of the labour market involves differentiated employment opportunities, benefits and salaries for nationals and expatriates. In GCC countries, according to the report, this differential is marked. In general, segmentation decreases mobility in the labour market, which brings down the productivity of the total workforce.[41]

Distorted wages and the non-wage benefits of public employees have, in turn, produced equally distorted salary expectations and increased unemployment in the Gulf monarchies. There is also simultaneously a greater share of women employed by and seeking employment in the public sector because of less discriminatory practices and a more standardised wage system than in the private sector in general. As a by-product of these tendencies, GCC countries have subsidised private-sector employment for national employees. According to the report, this has, however, only contributed to maintaining the expectations of high salaries among the nationals of these countries. When people decide to pursue higher education in order to qualify for well-paid government jobs, that in the past were practically guaranteed to graduates of higher education, this feeds to a growing bureaucracy and not to a market economy, says the report.[42]

The World Bank report cites the expansion of higher education, the high proportion of humanities and literature graduates and the slow rate of industrialisation as the causes of unemployment among the highly educated in the MENA region. However, according to the report, in oil-producing MENA countries, more education usually reduces the probability of unemployment.[43] Unemployment among the academically educated (percentage of unemployed) in GCC countries in fact remained at a lower level than in the OECD countries (30 per cent in 2003) but somewhat higher than in Latin America and the Caribbean (13 per cent in 1999). The most recent available figures, however, serve to demonstrate the differences between Gulf states: Bahrain 20 per cent (2004), Kuwait 6 per cent (2004), Oman 4 per cent (1996), Qatar 22 per cent (1997), Saudi Arabia 40 per cent (2005) and the UAE 20 per cent (1995). The fact that, according to the World Bank World Development Indicator statistics, 20 per cent of all those unemployed in Saudi Arabia were highly educated individuals in 2002 – half of the per centage in 2005 – paints a worrying picture in the case of this country, though it is also an indicator of how statistical data can change within a short range of time, for whatever reason. At the same time, female unemployment among the academically educated (percentage of unemployed females) has remained several times higher than male unemployment in most of the GCC countries: Bahrain 30 per cent (2004), Kuwait 11 per cent (2004), Oman 5 per cent (1996), Qatar 40 per cent (1997), Saudi Arabia 50 per cent (2002) and the UAE 49 per cent (1995).[44]

According to the report, women's participation in the labour force began to rise rapidly in the 1990s, one factor being the increase in the investment in women's education.[45] Women's participation has been consistently lower in GCC countries than in other MENA countries, although the differences have diminished in recent years.[46] By 2003, 20 to 24 per cent of women were working in Bahrain, Kuwait, Oman and Saudi Arabia, and 15 to 18 per cent in Qatar and the UAE. In the same year, the MENA average was 25 per cent. Nevertheless, the entire region still lags behind other developing regions in workforce gender parity. In Latin America a third (35 per cent) and in East Asia closer to half (42 per cent) of women were working in 2003.[47] A striking fact is that despite the increasing proportions of women in tertiary education and with academic degrees, women in Gulf states have still not fully managed to work their way into the active labour force.

Old Roads, New Roads, New Highways?

The Road Not Traveled concludes by observing that innovative educational reforms in the MENA region remain 'partial and timid' and that 'a more rapid pace of reform is a must'.[48] As this chapter has pointed out, this was probably true even in the GCC countries prior to 2003, when the period of observation included in the report ends. When compared with other MENA countries, GCC countries fared better according to some indicators, but ranked worse according to others. The comparison with the other MENA countries did not set the GCC far apart in the general picture, and in some areas important differences were observed among the Gulf monarchies. The fact that the World Bank report occasionally pays little or no attention to the GCC countries does not therefore seem to constitute a problem for the internal validity of the study. What the report is not able to grasp, however, due to its limited timescale, are the extent and the pace of the educational reforms currently taking place in this sub-region. Not only have these developments been insufficiently covered by the World Bank, but they also have gone largely unnoticed in other international organisations and in the rest of the world, with the exception of some of the most extravagant initiatives.

The World Bank report does not paint a very different forecast for the development of knowledge economies in GCC countries from those of the MENA region as a whole. The rapidly growing divergences in socio-economic growth and educational systems between the Gulf monarchies and the rest of the MENA do, however, urgently call for renewed attention from the relevant international and regional organisations in order to understand the extent and direction of these changes. Only then can these institutions provide Gulf states with appropriate and functional policy recommendations. *The Road Not Traveled* reminds us that 'the relationship between human capital and economic growth is highly conditioned by the quality and distribution of education in the labour force and the economic structure of each country' and that related policies also play an important role in this.[49] These challenges, which most of the MENA countries are only starting to confront, are already being addressed by the GCC states. Better equipped, in terms of both economic resources and stability – for the time being – to answer the global challenges of higher education, the Gulf Cooperation Council states are no longer on the road of reforms. They are already accelerating along the highway.

Notes

1. The UNESCO World Conference on Higher Education in the Twenty-first Century, Paris 1998 and the UNESCO Meeting of Higher Education Partners (World Conference on Higher Education +5), Paris 2003.
2. In the Arab context, the most important contribution has been the UNDP *Arab Human Development Report* of 2003.
3. For example, the Partnerships for Education, a joint initiative of the World Economic Forum and UNESCO, launched in 2007.
4. UNESCO, *World Declaration on Higher Education for the Twenty-first Century: vision and action, and framework for priority action for change and development in higher education,* Paris 1998.
5. UNDP, *Arab Human Development Report 2003: building a knowledge society,* Amman 2003, pp. 1–13.
6. World Bank, *The Road Not Traveled: education reform in the Middle East and North Africa,* Washington DC 2008.
7. *The Road Not Traveled,* p. 2.
8. On its website the World Bank includes in the MENA region the following countries/territories: Algeria, Bahrain, Djibouti, Egypt, Iran, Iraq, Israel, Jordan, Kuwait, Lebanon, Libya, Malta, Morocco, Oman, Qatar, Saudi Arabia, Syria, Tunisia, the United Arab Emirates, the West Bank and Gaza and Yemen. *The Road Not Traveled,* however, does not mention Malta and refers to Israel only once, from which it can be deduced that these countries are not included in the definition of MENA in the report. For the World Bank definition of the MENA region elsewhere, see: http://go.worldbank.org/7UEP77ZCB0.
9. *The Road Not Traveled,* pp. 1–2.
10. Ibid., pp. 2, 39, 110–11.
11. Ibid., pp. 117, 119–200.
12. Ibid., p. 4.

13. See, for example ibid., pp. 33–4, 203.
14. Ibid., p. 298.
15. One reason for the lesser attention might be the fact that the World Bank has concentrated almost exclusively on providing technical assistance to the GCC; presumably it therefore has less expertise on these countries than those in the rest of the MENA region.
16. See *The Road Not Traveled*, pp. 156–7, 162. A disclaimer on p. ii also states that '(e)ducation data during this period (1970–2003) for Saudi Arabia might underestimate the recent achievements in the country. New data ... using a new methodology show significantly positive differences over previous years.'
17. In many sections it is unclear which countries the authors have used as a basis for their arguments, and in others, even while the countries included are specified, the authors have chosen to continue using the term MENA, probably in order to maintain as wide a scope as possible for the subsequent policy recommendations. For examples, see ibid., pp. 24–6, 56–9, 61–3, 67–8, 223–4.
18. The averages of Latin America and East Asia presented in the report are similarly based on a sample of a few countries from each region.
19. *The Road Not Traveled*, pp. 10–11.
20. Ibid., pp. 47, 52.
21. Ibid., pp. 13, 15, 318. However, the report does not take into account the possible changes over the last five years, from 2003 to 2008.
22. Ibid., p. 21. Figures for Kuwait were not available. The country-specific percentages were: Bahrain 60.0, Oman 75.3, Qatar 67.4, Saudi Arabia 75.8 and the UAE 71.4. The figures are from 2002 and 2003, except for Saudi Arabia, the percentage of which is from 1996.
23. Ibid., p. 22.
24. Ibid., pp. 33–4. In addition to the fields of study, the indicators used to measure quality of human capital were scores on international tests (TIMSS [Trends in International Mathematics and Science Study test] and PISA [The OECD Programme for International Student Assessment]) and literacy rates.
25. Ibid., p. 34.
26. Ibid.
27. World Bank, *Knowledge Assessment Methodology, KEI and KI Indexes*, 2007. The index is composed of four pillars: economic incentive and institutional regime, education and human resources, the innovation system and information and communication technology. A total of eighty-three structural and qualitative variables are used in the measurement.
28. UN, *United Nations Common Database,* Population total (UN Population Division's annual estimates and projections), 2008. Here, the same countries were included in the MENA as in *The Road Not Traveled*.
29. *The Road Not Traveled*, pp. 31, 96.

30.   Ibid., pp. 95–9.
31.   Ibid., p. 167. The indicators compiled were as follows: for *access*, net enrol-
      ment rates for primary education and gross enrolment rates for secondary
      and higher education; for *quality*, literacy rates and TIMSS test scores; for
      equity, gender parity index and the Gini coefficients of the average years
      of schooling; and for *efficiency*, primary school completion rates. These
      indicators were normalised and all received a scale from 0 to 1.
32.   Ibid., pp. 168–70, 318.
33.   Ibid., pp. 171–3, 323.
34.   Ibid., p. 23. Where Middle Eastern and North African countries have
      raised their adult literacy rate from 50 per cent in 1980 to 78 per cent in
      2000–2004, the GCC countries have improved from 60 per cent to 85 per
      cent. The most impressive improvement has been made in Oman where
      only 36 per cent of the population aged fifteen and over was literate in 1980
      and where, two decades later the rate had risen to 81 per cent. Even though
      starting with notably lower initial rates in 1980, both MENA and GCC
      figures are still lagging behind East Asia (91 per cent total adult literacy in
      2000–2004) and Latin America (92 per cent).
35.   Ibid.
36.   Ibid., pp. 173–5.
37.   Ibid., pp. 80, 178–80, quotes from p. 179.
38.   Ibid., pp. 191–8, 203.
39.   Ibid., p. 211.
40.   Ibid, pp. 225–6.
41.   Ibid., pp. 225, 228.
42.   Ibid., pp. 227–8.
43.   Ibid., pp. 213–14.
44.   World Bank, *World Development Indicators*, 2007. Data for the entire MENA
      region were not available. The unemployment rates of the highly educated
      for some of the GCC countries were only available for the 1990s. General
      unemployment in the GCC countries remained below the MENA average
      of 15 per cent (2003) during the first half of the 2000s, the rates being as
      follows: Bahrain 5 (2001), Kuwait 2 (2004), Qatar 4 (2001), Saudi Arabia
      5 (2002), and the UAE 2 per cent (2000). Here, data for Oman were not
      available.
45.   *The Road Not Traveled*, p. 221.
46.   *World Development Indicators*. In 1980, only 5 to 8 per cent of women in
      Oman, Qatar, Saudi Arabia and the UAE, and 11 to 13 per cent in Bahrain
      and Kuwait participated in the workforce while the MENA average was 18
      per cent.
47.   *The Road Not Traveled*, p. 222.
48.   Ibid., p. 298.
49.   Ibid., p. 75.

THREE

Policy Politics of Higher Education in the Gulf Cooperation Council Member States: intersections of globality, regionalism and locality [1]

André Elias Mazawi

The study of higher education in Gulf Cooperation Council (GCC) member states remains a neglected area despite dynamic expansion in one of the world's strategic regions. The patterns of expansion are telling. From one higher education institution in the Arabian Peninsula surveyed by Jean-Jacques Waardenburg in the 1960s,[2] official GCC statistics for 2003 place the total number of higher education students at about 661,000, of whom at least 60 per cent are women. The same statistics indicate that the total number of faculty members stands at over 30,000, of whom around 40 per cent are women, significant differences between states and across types of institution and disciplinary fields notwithstanding.[3] This expansion bears testimony to the role educational credentials have played in GCC societies since the early 1990s, following the Gulf war. The expansion of higher education underscores the centrality of educational credentials as forms of social and political capital which are mobilised to secure access to public service positions and to positions of status and power more generally. Credentials also provide state-entrenched elites with new mechanisms to co-opt and control emerging middle classes and professional constituencies.[4] The distributive role of the state, in what are rentier economies, also means that reforms in GCC higher education, and the introduction of Information and Communication Technology (ICT), are sensitive to considerations associated with the containment of political discontent, particularly with regard to the younger generations.[5]

Yet, despite the expansion of GCC higher education, few attempts have been undertaken to examine its broader implications for the emergence of new centres of power and authority, either in GCC societies or for expatriate workers drawn into higher education institutions. Even fewer research efforts have been invested with the view of examining the impact of higher education expansion on the capacity of GCC member states to manoeuvre or otherwise negotiate the turbulent geopolitical and global contingencies within which they operate, particularly in the period following the Gulf war of 1990–1991.

In the present chapter, the expansion of higher education in GCC member states is not viewed as exclusively limited to nation-building policies anchored in human capital development.[6] Nor is it viewed as exclusively confined to processes associated with social mobility and class differentiation within Gulf societies.[7] Rather, the expansion of higher education – and particularly the university sector – reflects, in addition, the outcome of multifaceted processes situated at the juncture of global, geo-regional and national dynamics that intersect in various and complex ways. It is useful to point out that, for instance, as part of this process, Egyptian and other Arab universities gradually lost their position as major socialisers and suppliers of prospective faculty members to the GCC region from the late 1980s onwards. They were gradually supplanted by faculty members who are more often graduates of American, British and other Western universities. This change is considerable in its implications. Facilitated by 'educational diplomacy' of Western governments, other regional blocs and Western academic institutions, this process is accompanied by economic restructuring promoted by Gulf governments, in their attempts to diversify their economies and increase the share of the private sector in their national labour markets.

Currently, GCC higher education systems are being structurally 'synchronised' with their US counterparts, in terms of accreditation and curricula, leading James Coffman to state that the American academic model 'rules supreme' in Gulf universities.[8] Describing a new GCC university, one American consultant observed that:

> (The University) is being designed to reflect the typical design of colleges and universities in the US so it will qualify for accreditation – or its equivalent – by regional and professional accrediting associations in the US. That, in sum, will facilitate transfers to US institutions and entrance to US graduate programmes for students with those aspirations.[9]

Accreditation with higher education institutions operating in other Arab states (or even within the GCC region) is not raised as part of these structural reforms. Instead, one notices a discourse grounded in competition, an almost 'all against all' war of sorts, between GCC member states – and in the United Arab Emirates (UAE), also between emirates – in their efforts to draw into their respective territories higher education programmes and fully-fledged campuses operated by US, British, Australian and other universities. The GCC region has become an arena where competitive corporate actors vie aggressively for profit and for a greater share of revenues, in an ever expanding market of educational commodities.[10]

Some writers view the restructuring of GCC higher education as part of attempts to 'shift ... the intellectual heart of the Middle East', by transforming the GCC states into a 'regional hub' of world-class higher education providers, thus eclipsing the position of veteran higher learning centres operating in Beirut, Cairo, Damascus or Baghdad.[11] Others argue that higher education expansion in the GCC region reflects broader processes of globalisation and internationalisation of higher education, similar to those occurring in other world regions.[12] Yet one should also carefully examine how the introduction of new academic models plays a crucial role in mediating regional economic and political realignments across the GCC and the larger Arab region.[13] This aspect acquires particular importance given the competition between the US and the European Union (EU) in their efforts to exert influence over what they consider as a strategic region, vital to the conduct of their foreign policies.[14] For instance, some European policy strategists identify the GCC region as an important asset for the EU, both politically and in terms of the development of 'commercial' higher education ventures. However, they do admit that, compared with their US counterparts, 'European educational institutions are simply absent from the region.' They therefore strongly recommend that the 'EU should aim at establishing at least one European University in each of the GCC member countries, in cooperation with major European universities', as part of 'a specific goal of the Union'.[15] Initiatives in this direction have already taken place, with Paris-Sorbonne launching its first campus in the UAE.

Within this broader context, the growth in the number of GCC private institutions has been striking, in terms of both institutional types and scope of programmes offered. Nevertheless, since the early 1990s, the greater role played by private and semi-private investment agencies in higher education plays out differently across the GCC region. While these regional investments aim to restructure the economy and the labour market, and eventually lessen reliance on imported workers, their strategies are not without challenges or difficulties.[16] GCC governments have set up semi-public multi-billion-dollar foundations – for instance, the Qatar Foundation – to promote the reforming and the privatisation of schooling and higher education offerings in their countries.

The growing privatisation of higher education is particularly noticeable in the number of higher education institutions in most GCC countries, with the exception of Saudi Arabia where educational provision remains still largely controlled by the state. For instance, in 2006, only two out of eleven universities operating in the UAE were public and one out of eight universities and colleges in Kuwait. Even GCC states which started their higher education systems relatively more recently, such as Oman (its first university was launched in the mid-1980s), currently rely extensively on privately run universities in expanding access opportunities, with only one out of four universities being public in 2006. Effectively, the Omani state relies on private higher education, in conjunction with international providers. The latter offer their programmes according to the American credits system, and with English as the primary 'medium and language of instruction'.[17] Regarding private institutions which operate on a for-profit basis, Salma al-Lamki poignantly observes that they 'are not addressing the academic needs of the society. They have commercialized education into a commodity that can be bought or sold in the market.'[18] She therefore wonders whether, despite this impressive expansion, 'the masses will have the financial means to cater for their education. This includes poor students, working class with low income, and many secondary school graduates in provinces with no tertiary level offerings.'[19] Similar concerns have also been expressed with regard to higher education expansion and diversification policies implemented in the UAE and Qatar, where private higher education institutions have witnessed a dramatic surge.[20]

Still, Saudi Arabia – which operates the largest higher education system in the GCC region – follows a somewhat different trajectory. With eight public universities and eight additional public ones under advanced planning or under construction, in addition to colleges and institutes, the state's involvement in building and operating higher education institutions remains considerable, despite the emergence of a sector of locally-run 'private' university colleges.[21] Thus, as the first decade of the twenty-first century draws to its close, Saudi Arabia and the other GCC member states are following policy trajectories which differ in some respects, with the latter granting a greater share to campuses directly established by foreign universities. These trajectories are consequential in terms of their impact on the articulation of regional GCC higher education policies, an aspect I return to below. Here, suffice it to note that the consequences are not only institutional or structural, in terms of higher education opportunities offered to students, but also socio-political, in terms of the emphases students and faculty are exposed to.

The expansion of higher education provision has also been affected by policies which aim to establish more explicit linkages to the labour market and more particularly to jobs in the private sector. Efforts in this direction have led some senior policy makers to call for a 'review (of) the existing "open door" admission policy' into public higher education and for a greater emphasis on the preparation of professionals and technicians.[22] Particularly, technology colleges and institutes – which offer specialisations within post-secondary vocational education – were introduced in view of reconfiguring the interface between education and work and facilitate the transition of citizens into the labour market.[23] These venues do not necessarily lessen the reliance of GCC countries on expatriate workers, however. For instance, with regard to Saudi Arabia, Mellahi observes that colleges of technology face considerable difficulties in attracting citizens into 'non-office skilled jobs such as mechanic and production engineering' because they 'overwhelmingly prefer specialties that have white collar jobs prospects'.[24] Other initiatives, for instance in Qatar, the UAE and Kuwait, led to the establishing of hi-tech industrial and science 'incubators', often attached to free zones, in an attempt to enhance research and development and the capabilities of the private sector, and generate occupational opportunities for qualified citizens. In the UAE, the launching in 2003 of Dubai's Knowledge Village (located in the Dubai Technology and Media Free Zone) aimed 'to create a modern, vibrant learning environment' and 'a critical mass for the new economy' with over '50 educational and research institutions as partners'[25] offering '100-per cent repatriation of assets and profits, tax free'.[26] Similarly, in Qatar, the creation of Education City aims to attract leading US universities and diversify the offerings of educational programmes in a variety of fields perceived as facilitating the emergence of a skilled and competitive labour force fit for a 'knowledge economy'. This said, one wonders whether through these and other initiatives the GCC region is not becoming a consumer of knowledge, technologies and learning packages produced elsewhere, with only limited relevance for local society and economic growth.

Issues of higher education development in the GCC region are tightly linked to demographic issues, given the number of GCC citizens in relation to expatriate and the barring of expatriate workers from accessing citizenship. In the longer term, member states may have to reconsider their citizenship policies, and revise higher education reforms in ways which target not only their limited pool of citizens, but the larger pool of expatriate workers and students from outside the GCC region, if governments wish to develop a sustainable higher education infrastructure and facilitate the emergence of a locally-engaged and locally-invested 'knowledge economy'. Though sporadic, some statements to that effect have already been made. For instance, a UAE education official recently recognised that, for current higher education policies to bear meaningful fruits, efforts should also be made to cater for the educational and professional needs of expatriate workers who contribute to the country.[27]

Investments in higher education benefit significantly from revenues generated by oil exports, allowing for developments, particularly in the fields of science and technology. Moreover, higher education institutions which offer learning opportunities beyond the conventional university campuses have also emerged across the GCC region. This is particularly the case of distance education venues, which were traditionally perceived as accommodating mainly women.[28] Since then, distance education has expanded considerably, in diverse formats, to include working individuals, including expatriate workers. For instance, the Arab Open University (AOU), launched with the support of the Arab Gulf Fund for United Nations Development Organisations (AGFUND), currently operates in conjunction with Britain's Open University. Plans are reportedly underway to expand its activity across the Arab region. Yet, according to Amel Ahmed Hassan Mohamed, this cooperation is 'leaving no room to develop home-grown materials'.[29] Moreover, distance education venues (including open universities) are still perceived as distinct forms of higher education, leaving issues associated with the transfer of students into regular universities and the labour market largely unresolved, if not particularly challenging for graduates.

At the institutional level, the organisation of the GCC academic workplace exhibits deeply entrenched cleavages in terms of the distribution of faculty members, along nationality, social class, gender and types of credentials obtained.[30] First, GCC universities – public and private – overwhelmingly depend on migrant academic labour, to varying degrees, less in Saudi Arabia compared with other GCC states. The three major groups of expatriate academics – holding Arab, Asian–African and Western nationalities – are differentially distributed across GCC states, universities and across disciplinary fields within institutions, suggesting an 'ethnic' division of labour which often intersects with gender and types of credentials held by faculty members.

For instance, in Saudi Arabia, my analyses of faculty member demographics and distribution across disciplinary fields in the late 1990s suggest that the intersection between gender and institutional location of faculty members is mediated by type of credentials held: Saudi Arabian citizens who hold local doctorates are more likely to be employed as faculty members in either the Islamic universities or in the humanities in non-Islamic universities. Saudi Arabian women who graduate from local universities are more likely to be employed in the humanities and social sciences in non-Islamic universities. Other fields in the sciences are stratified, too, mostly with faculty members from outside the Arab region.

GCC national women working in higher education, particularly in Saudi Arabia, are in a position of 'double-minority': they navigate their way in relation both to national men and to expatriate academics. While the occupational integration of women is perceived as a venue through which the private sector could be bolstered, the diversification of the national economy pursued and reliance on oil rents and imported labour lessened, women's opportunities are too often carved in ways which do not challenge local cultural mores.[31] Nevertheless, since the outbreak of the 1990–1991 Gulf war women academics have been appointed to lead several Gulf universities, with the first appointment undertaken in Kuwait in 1994. Since then, appointments have facilitated women's access to ministerial positions in education, higher education and scientific research institutions. Some writers suggest that these processes reflect the larger debates currently taking place in GCC societies around what is labelled as the 'woman question'. Within the broader socio-political and economic contexts of the region, the 'question' has become considerably 'politicised' in terms of its articulations in relation to the legitimacy of the state, conceptions of citizenship and participation in public affairs.[32]

Second, GCC higher education institutions are 'territorialised' spaces. Contrary to migrant academic labour, GCC citizens are much more likely to be employed within their country's universities and much less often in other GCC institutions of higher education. Thus, regional pools of academic labour and regional competition over academic positions remain confined, if not non-existent, as far as Gulf citizens are concerned. This is reinforced by state-level policies which seek to recruit academics from among citizens. The establishment of regional universities, such as the Arabian Gulf University (AGU) in Bahrain in the early 1980s, did not lead to a significant increase in the mobility of GCC nationals across the region, as faculty members, despite schemes for faculty and student exchange and despite efforts to coordinate higher education policies through the Arab Bureau of Education for the Gulf States (ABEGS). More recently, calls for a regional policy review have been made, with the aim of articulating clearer linkages and greater cooperation among GCC higher education systems. While this would require greater coordination with regard to accreditation and transfer, this policy could, if reviewed, help scaffold an eventual GCC 'academic region' which would enhance the mobility of faculty and students across the region. Nevertheless, the state of GCC and inter-Arab cooperation in the field of higher education is of particular concern. Regional educational agencies do not enjoy a binding role at this time, and a concerted and pro-active regional policy on higher education remains largely lacking. Existing policies and agreements are only loosely coupled with GCC regional dynamics and labour market flows as well as with other higher education systems across the Arab region. For the observer, this state of affairs raises serious concerns over the contributions of higher education initiatives currently taking place in the GCC region in terms of promoting a viable regional academic sphere. The lack of a regional policy, precisely under conditions of spiralling investments in 'national' schemes through the private (international) sector, may prove to exacerbate regional 'implosion', carried under the weight of generalised competition in the field of higher education.

Moreover, in considering a GCC 'academic region', it is important to ponder on the implications of the synchronisation of GCC higher education institutions along the models prevalent in American universities and colleges. The synchronisation is setting higher education institutions in the GCC region apart from their counterparts operating across the Arab region, and in some cases even within the GCC.[33] This aspect may affect more particularly the mobility of graduates of Arab universities – recruited as faculty members, policymakers or educational leaders into the GCC region. A 'closed market' of sorts may be gradually reinforced, offering stratified mobility and work opportunities to academics educated and trained outside the region, in Western universities, compared with their counterparts who graduate from Arab universities.

Two interrelated policy areas, briefly signalled here for reflection, deserve further exploration; their discussion clearly goes beyond the scope of the present chapter. First, contemplating a GCC 'academic region' requires a holistic approach that considers higher education in relation to political, economic and socio-cultural dynamics. Policies in this direction should be sensitive to intra- and inter-regional spatial dynamics in negotiating the contradictory and ever-changing demands placed on higher education. This means approaching the notion of a GCC 'academic region' as a multilayered and multifaceted construct that articulates sustainable linkages to institutions operating at the local, regional, Arab and global levels. A one-dimensional synchronisation of GCC higher education institutions, along a particular academic model of delivery, as is currently the case, renders the GCC vulnerable and a hostage of a conjunctural configuration of economic and political circumstances. On the one hand, a viable notion of a GCC 'academic region' has to clarify the role multilateral agreements can play in creating regional pools of opportunities for students and faculty, as well as in promoting opportunities for research engagement that would provide new spaces for GCC public and private higher education institutions in contributing to regional development.[34] On the other hand, GCC states must consider the effects of uncoordinated intra-regional expansion when developing 'magnet' higher education opportunities which would ultimately deepen the dependency of all GCC member states on outside providers.

The second policy area, interrelated with the first, focuses on the intersection of higher education and citizenship. As pointed out earlier, the expansion of higher education opportunities, and the spread of credentialism in GCC societies, cannot be seen as sheer 'human capital' development strategies which lead to 'development' in an automatic fashion. Rather, the effects of credentialism – and its identity and civic correlates – go farther than that. They intersect with culture, religion and political participation in the conduct of public affairs. In a sense, the expansion of higher education implies the transformation of the public sphere and the re-configuration of the bases of social and political authority which sustain its legitimacy. Hence, understanding the role higher education plays in broader processes of social and economic development requires an understanding of the contribution of higher education to the articulation of new sources of authority and legitimacy which require their own spaces of social, political and economic action in relation to which they can meaningfully operate.

Notes

1. The present chapter draws and builds on my work on GCC higher education published during the years 2003 to 2007 and more particularly on the following studies: 'The Academic Workplace in Arab Gulf Public Universities', in P. G. Altbach, ed., *The Decline of the Guru: the academic profession in developing and middle-income countries*, New York 2003, pp. 231–69; 'Divisions of Academic Labor: nationals and non-nationals in Arab Gulf universities', in *International Journal of Contemporary Sociology*, no. 40, 2003, pp. 91–110; 'Contrasting Perspectives on Higher Education Governance in the Arab States', in *Higher Education: handbook of theory and research*, no. 20, 2005, pp. 133–89; 'The Academic Profession in a Rentier State: the case of the Saudi Arabian professoriate', in *Minerva: a review of science, learning and policy*, no. 43, 2005, pp. 221–4; 'State Power, Faculty Recruitment and the Emergence of Constituencies in Saudi Arabia', in R. Griffin, ed., *Education in the Muslim World: different perspectives – an overview*, Oxford 2006, pp. 55–78; 'Besieging the King's Tower? En/gendering Academic Opportunities in the Gulf Arab States', in C. Brock and L. Zia Levers, eds, *Aspects of Education in the Middle East and North Africa*, Oxford 2007, pp. 77–97.
2. Jean-Jacques Waardenburg, *Les Universités dans le monde arabe actuel*, vols I & II, Paris and La Haye 1966.
3. Refer to the statistics section of the GCC General Secretariat website: <http://www.gccsg.org>.
4. For instance, with regard to the role post-secondary educational credentials play in Saudi Arabia, see: Richard H. Dekmejian, 'Saudi Arabia's Consultative Council', in *Middle East Journal*, no. 52, 1998, pp. 204–18; Madawi al-Rasheed, *Contesting the Saudi State: Islamic voices from a new generation*, Cambridge 2007, pp. 61–5.
5. Emma Murphy, 'Agency and Space: the political impact of information technologies in the Gulf Arab states', in *Third World Quarterly*, no. 27, 2006, pp. 1059–83; Daryl Champion, *The Paradoxical Kingdom: Saudi Arabia and the momentum of reform*, New York 2003, pp. 113–20.
6. Refer to the various contributions in K. E. Shaw, ed., *Higher Education in the Gulf: problems and prospects*, Exeter 1997. Refer also to the contributions in *Education and the Arab World: challenges of the next millennium*, Abu Dhabi 2000 and to my review of the book published in *Discourse: studies in the cultural politics of education*, no. 23, 2001, pp. 396–404.
7. Champion, pp. 114–19.
8. James Coffman, 'Higher Education in the Gulf: privatization and Americanization', in *International Higher Education*, no. 33, 2003, pp. 17–19.

9. William F. Halloran, 'Zayed University: a new model for higher education', in *Education and the Arab World*, pp. 323–30. Cited on pp. 329–30.

10. Paul Lefrere, 'Competing Higher Education Futures in a Globalising World', in *European Journal of Education*, no. 42, 2007, pp. 201–22. See pp. 209–11.

11. Zvika Krieger, 'Desert Boom', in *The Chronicle of Higher Education*, vol. 54, no. 29, 28 March 2008, p. B7.

12. Lefrere, pp. 209–11.

13. For instance, on the political role played by American academic models introduced in South America, see Philip G. Altbach, 'Education and Neo-colonialism', in B. Ashcroft, G. Griffiths and H. Tiffin, eds, *The Post-Colonial Studies Reader*, London and New York 2005, pp. 452–56. See p. 455.

14. See, for instance, Völker Perthes, 'America's "Greater Middle East" and Europe: key issues for dialogue', in *Middle East Policy*, no. 11, 2004, pp. 85–97.

15. Giacomo Luciani and Felix Neugart, eds, *The EU and the GCC: a new partnership*, Munich 2005, pp. 25, 26.

16. On expatriate workers in the GCC member states refer to: Andrzej Kapiszewski, *Nationals and Expatriates: population and labour dilemmas of the Gulf Cooperation Council states*, Reading 2001.

17. Salma al-Lamki, 'The Development of Private Higher Education in the Sultanate of Oman: perception and analysis', in *International Journal of Private Education*, no. 1, 2006, pp. 54–77. Accessible online at <http://www.xaiu.edu.cn/xaiujournal>. Cited on p. 62.

18. Ibid., p. 64.

19. Ibid., p. 65.

20. Timothy N. Walters, Alma Kadragic and Lynne M. Walters, 'Miracle or Mirage: is development sustainable in the United Arab Emirates?', in *The Middle East Review of International Affairs*, no. 10, 2006, pp. 77–91. Accessible online at: <http://meria.idc.ac.il/journal/previousj.html>; Joan Muysken and Samia Nour, 'Deficiencies in Education and Poor Prospects for Economic Growth in the Gulf Countries: the case of the UAE', in *Journal of Development Studies*, no. 42, 2006, pp. 957–80.

21. One should none the less note that Saudi Arabia has witnessed the expansion of what are often described as 'community institutions' of higher education (*mu'asasat ahliyah*). While these institutions often involve various forms of partnerships or consultancies with US universities, their operation remains much more limited in comparison with the number of state-operated institutions. For reasons of space, this aspect of the Saudi Arabian higher education system is not discussed here in more detail. See Amani Hamdan, 'Women and Education in Saudi Arabia: challenges and achievements', in *International Education Journal*, no. 6, 2005, pp. 42–54. Accessible online at: <http://ehlt.flinders.edu.au/education/iej/articles/v6n1/hamdan/paper.>

pdf>. See, more particularly, p. 52.

22.   Hamad Al-Sulayti, 'Education and Training in the GCC countries: some issues of concern', in *Education and the Arab World*, pp. 271–8.

23.   Stephen Wilkins, 'Human Resource Development through Vocational Education in the United Arab Emirates: the case of Dubai Polytechnic', in *Journal of Vocational Education and Training*, no. 54, 2002, pp. 5–26.

24.   Kamel Mellahi, 'Human Resource Development through Vocational Education in Gulf Cooperation Countries: the case of Saudi Arabia', in *Journal of Vocational Education and Training*, no. 52, 2000, pp. 329–44, cited in pp. 337–8. See also Champion.

25.   Walters, Kadragic and Walters, p. 80.

26.   Zvika Krieger, 'An Academic Building Boom Transforms the Persian Gulf', in *The Chronicle of Higher Education*, no. 29, vol. 54, 2008, p. A26.

27.   Ibid.

28.   Haya Saad Al-Rawaf and Cyril Simmons, 'Distance Higher Education for Women in Saudi Arabia: present and proposed', in *Distance Education*, no. 13, 1992, pp. 65–80; S. H. Shaker, 'Distance Education in Bahrain: situation and needs', in *Open Learning*, no. 15, 2000, pp. 57–70.

29.   Amel Ahmed Hassan Mohamed, 'Distance Higher Education in the Arab Region: the need for quality assurance frameworks', in *Online Journal of Distance Learning Administration*, no. 3, 2005. Available at: <http://www.westga.edu/~distance/ojdla/spring81/mohamed81.htm>.

30.   For this part of the discussion, see my publications listed in note 1, above.

31.   Dawn Chatty, 'Women Working in Oman: individual choice and cultural constraints', in *International Journal of Middle East Studies*, no. 32, 2000, pp. 241–54 and Amani Hamdan.

32.   See, for example, Eleanor Abdella Doumato, 'Education in Saudi Arabia: gender, jobs, and the price of religion', in E. A. Doumato and M. P. Posusney, eds, *Women and Globalization in the Arab Middle East*, Boulder 2003, pp. 239–57.

33.   The American credits system has gained ground across the Arab region. Notwithstanding, Arab higher education institutions still differ in terms of their academic models, sometimes within the same state. On the whole Maghrib universities follow the French academic model. Middle East universities follow a composite academic model which combines, in different ways, the Continental model and elements of the American credits model. Some countries, such as Lebanon, operate mostly private universities which follow different academic models. See Munir Bashshur, *Higher Education in the Arab States*, Beirut 2004.

34.   The disconnect between GCC higher education institutions and the broader process of development is associated with an overwhelming reliance on foreign consultancies and expertise.

FOUR

Institutionalising Charisma: comparative perspectives on the promise of higher education

Gregory Starrett

> No fallacy is more transparent or more monstrous than that which assumes that knowledge, or whatever training is got in schools, is a natural want, certain to assert itself like the want of food, or clothing, or shelter, and to create a demand. The fact is the very reverse of this assumption. All statesmen who have wished to civilize and instruct a nation have had to create this appetite.[1]

The stunning expansion of education in the Gulf states has drawn international attention as a grandly scaled but perhaps otherwise rather commonsense and narrowly technical exercise in national manpower planning and institutional development. Questions of quality assurance, programme funding, curriculum design, facilities planning, faculty recruitment, student support and career guidance, and other familiar staples of educational administration appear vital to the future of these states as they wrestle with the concept of 'human capital' during the long, slow dawn of the post-oil economy. But it is worth recalling that programmes of mass formal schooling, as a means of producing particular kinds of citizens, are relatively recent on a global scale. They emerged not only from the economic crucible of early nineteenth-century industrial capitalism but from a peculiar set of assumptions about the nature of domestic social relationships, international politics and knowledge itself. In this chapter I would like to explore the historical context of education in the Middle East more generally as a way to illuminate the contemporary educational efforts of GCC countries as outlined in this book's other chapters.

The histories and contemporary dynamics of higher education in the region have included a series of alliances and conflicts between particular interest groups, including royal families, military establishments, urban merchants, foreign colonial administrators, peasant villages and the educated elites of the nascent middle and professional classes themselves. But those histories also include encounters and conflicts between distinctly different kinds of authority and power. Just prior to the First World War, German sociologist Max Weber wrote that authority could be understood as flowing from one of three sources: patriarchy, bureaucracy and charisma. Traditional, or patriarchal power, has as its model the kinship relationships within family, lineage, and village, 'resting ... on habit, respect for tradition, piety towards elders and ancestors and bonds of personal loyalty'.[2] Bureaucratic authority is the result of systems of training and certification, and relies on literacy skills, record-keeping, rational planning and the 'submission to deliberately created rules'.[3] Charismatic authority, finally, emerges from a sense on the part of ordinary people that a particular leader has supernatural gifts available only to a few. While rational bureaucracy creates change by enforcing rules, thereby revolutionising behaviour from the outside, charismatic authority 'exerts its revolutionary power from within, by producing a fundamental change of heart in the ruled ... Instead of the pious following of time-hallowed custom, it enforces inner subjection to something which has never before existed, is absolutely unique and is therefore considered divine.'[4]

For something more than 150 years, 'Education' has become conceptualised in both Europe and the Middle East as such a charismatic force. During the course of the nineteenth and early twentieth centuries education was both reified – turned from a heterogeneous set of ideas and practices into a seemingly independent force – and apotheosised, perceived and treated as a practice that could arguably achieve almost any end if designed and applied appropriately. Education as an idea came to possess the charisma that Weber had attributed to prophets. Rulers, educated elites and the population at large have been caught up in debating its promise ever since.

Education in Historical Context

James Kay-Shuttleworth's practical observation, above, about the source of interest in education reminds us that schooling, as we organise it, is a cultural practice with specific historical roots, rather than a necessary or natural response to the imperative of rearing children or solving social problems. While it is easy to highlight the role of the literate in maintaining and advancing complex civilisations, it is also the case that the vast majority of the world's civilisations have thrived with only tiny numbers of literate members, and that formal, institutionalised education is not the only way to transmit and develop skills and knowledge.

Nor has education always been seen as a means of personal advancement or increased status. Although Middle Eastern history and thought are full of high praise for learning and for men of knowledge, they also contain their share of cynical observations about the fate of the educated and the quality of teachers. A thirteenth-century Persian joke describes a street performer threatening to abandon his lazy son to a *madrasa* 'to learn their dead and useless science and to become a scholar so as to live in contempt and misery and adversity and never be able to earn a penny wherever you go',[5] while Shalaby provides numerous examples of classical Arabic reflections on the ignorance and low status of schoolteachers.[6] The pious formulae recited by contemporary educators and politicians regarding the promise of

particular educational strategies or outcomes has been matched both by
blistering cynicism towards 'Edumania ... this hitherto unknown mental
disorder ... common in Cairo and Alexandria whose ... inhabitants seem
to be desperately intent on pushing their reluctant offspring into the
diplomatic corps',[7] and by the depressing recognition that education is
not always correlated with humanistic ideals, personal enlightenment
and progressive social change.[8]

The word 'education' is often derived from the Latin *educare*,
'to rear or raise', and has been used in English since the sixteenth
century to refer to the care and training of both animals and humans.
This might indicate either very specific sorts of skills training, as
when applied to horses or dogs, or the conscious development of
modes of thought, habits or even emotions and moral apprehension
thought appropriate to particular stations in life, when applied to
humans. In Arabic, two terms are often used to describe the process
of socialisation: *taʿlim* and *tarbiya*. *Taʿlim* refers to the process of
acquiring knowledge, and is often spoken of as a much more restricted
process than *tarbiya*, which denotes upbringing more generally, the
incorporation of moral qualities and proper behaviour through
interaction with family members.

The English word 'education' is associated also, though, with
the Latin *educere*, which means 'to lead out' or 'to draw out,' as in
leading a boat from harbour. In this second sense, education has been
thought of as a process of developing the personality, of drawing out
an essential self through programmes of instruction and discipline
which have the paradoxical effect of moulding the individual to the
social environment at the same time that they reveal an individual's
essence in its most highly evolved form. As one historian of higher
education has put it, from the perspective of most teaching faculty,
college education is meant not only to prepare students for jobs or
careers, but 'serves to liberate their souls' as well.[9]

Emphasis on the liberation of souls or the development of a
true self is both an idealist and an elitist notion. Historically, few
policymakers have expressed much interest, for example, in peasants

discovering their true selves independently of the social and economic function of the peasantry as a whole. It is far more common for leaders, particularly those working at national scales, to think of education in terms of two other sorts of goals, one political and the other moral. As far back as the beginning of the nineteenth century, as Benjamin Fortna has shown in his extraordinary book *Imperial Classroom*, formal education in its Western sense was seen by Middle Eastern leaders as an almost magical process through which a multitude of social and political goals could be pursued.[10] By the second decade of the nineteenth century, Ottoman and Qajar leaders had begun sending student missions to European countries to study the sciences of chemistry, metallurgy, geology, ballistics and mathematics, as well as European languages, translation and crafts like printing. The goal was overwhelmingly practical and targeted at building military strength. By the end of that century some other students were also studying European law, literature and political science, broadening the cultural and intellectual reach of the missions and preparing a generation of new intellectuals and technocrats with perspectives and interests different from those of other indigenous elites.[11]

The moral goal of education, on the other hand, concerned the creation and maintenance of cultural traditions and socio-political structures. Ottoman military officer Sulayman Pasha, reflecting in 1892 on the necessity of state-sponsored schools in the provinces along the Tigris and Euphrates, advised that:

> If the state establishes a teacher-training school in Baghdad right away, and later builds (elementary) schools in every town, village, and tax farming district, and thereafter establishes middle schools in the cities of Mosul, Kerkuk, Baghdad, and Basra, then the people educated there, being brought under the aegis of proper upbringing and education, will be in a position to benefit the state, and it will be able to be said of them that 'we have people who can distinguish between good and evil.' If not, they will be of no possible benefit to the state. On the one hand, they will remain shrouded by the nightmare of ignorance and on the other,

they will continue to be corrupted by the false principles of
their (Shi'i) spiritual leaders ... The expansion of education
will confirm their affinity to religion, fatherland, and
patriotism, and render sincere the bonds to our highness
the Caliph of the Muslims. But if ignorance continues, it will
intensify and aggravate the splitting apart and disintegration
(of those bonds).[12]

Education's role was simultaneously defensive (to protect Iraqi
Muslims from Shi'i propaganda from Iran or from local Shi'i leaders), constructive (creating bonds of loyalty to the Sultan and to the
empire) and developmental (to teach the people right from wrong
and rid them of ignorance). Significantly, Sulayman Pasha recommended that schools start with books in Arabic and Kurdish, and
then introduce books in Turkish with Arabic and Kurdish translations,
propelling local students into a closer linguistic connection with
the imperial core. 'So far as (the system) exhibited any considered
policy', Gertrude Bell wrote almost thirty years later, 'it was devised
to Ottomanize the Arabs.'[13]

By the time the British became Iraq's new masters during the First
World War, the entire curriculum was in Turkish, and Gertrude Bell
lamented that no Arabic-speaking teachers existed outside what she
called the '*mullah* schools'. Given that 'all sections of the population
wished their children to learn English for commercial purposes',
English was proposed as a language of instruction concurrent but
secondary to Arabic, as 'bait to attract boys to the government
primary schools'.[14] Lacking Arabic-speaking teachers trained in
modern subjects or in English, the new imperium contracted with
the American Mission School in Basra for training teachers and for
supervising the new government primary schools there.

The issue of language is strategic, of course, for both the sponsors
and the students in schools. Similar political considerations went
into educational planning in Egypt, in Morocco and elsewhere (in
1920s Uganda, for example, proposals to teach in Swahili instead of
English in Christian missionary schools were opposed by parents,

who were less concerned about national culture than with practical success, and felt their children would be locked out of good jobs without solid English-language education). In Morocco at the same time, the French encouraged Arabic-language schools along the coast, and French-language schools in the Berber highlands to prevent the country's ethnic and tribal networks from uniting against the colonial power. In Egypt, local schools under the British occupation were given government grants if they did not teach foreign languages – the goal was to keep peasants in their villages rather than aspiring to work in lettered occupations in the cities. Various logistical schemes, including the manipulation of rules regarding school fees and government salaries, were aimed at preventing rural–urban migration.[15] In some ways these were continuations of long-standing population policies under the Ottoman viceroy Muhammad Ali,[16] and regulated the number of Egyptian students who would enter the ladder of modern-style education and sever themselves from their parents' place and occupation. Much more recently in Algeria, the Arabisation of the formerly French-language public schools was at the centre of nationalist efforts to repudiate the colonial heritage, but has created new tensions between the country's Arab and Berber populations.[17] It has also threatened the international competitiveness and application of indigenous scientific research, which depends both on access to European languages and on the creation of local interest and experience with science at lower grades and in public culture at large.[18]

Schooling – all schooling, it should be remembered – is ultimately a form of social engineering, a complicated and usually troubled enterprise. When the task of that engineering is taken up by the very populations it creates – for example, the new classes of educated technocrats, including teachers, journalists, lawyers and other bureaucrats generated in new schools – the meaning of education begins to change. In Egypt, the graduates of new schools and alumni of foreign study missions formed the core of the nationalist movement of the late nineteenth and early twentieth centuries, first rebelling against British rule and then against the last of the Circassian dynasty in Cairo. Waves of anti-British riots in 1904 and 1919 were led by students.

Walter Armbrust, of Oxford University, has pointed out that Egyptian popular culture throughout most of the twentieth century has portrayed education as a path to a specific kind of modernity.[19] The universal extension of formal schooling would solve two social problems as they existed from the point of view of the slowly consolidating modern middle class. It would, first of all, transform the dissolute aristocracy of landowners, notables and Circassian elites into modern Egyptians who had a love for their country rather than their class, and who would use their wealth and knowledge to benefit society at large. Secondly, schooling would transform the backward peasantry by lifting them out of superstition and ignorance and poverty, adding loyalty to the nation to the loyalty they already felt to village and clan and family. This change would not take place at the expense of authentic Egyptian values and traditions, but would create a modern Egyptian citizen who was simultaneously a vessel of authentic values, and an engine of social and economic change. It is this central and contradictory promise that is one of the most important issues for us to deal with when thinking about the purpose and the effect of higher education.

Armbrust traces the ways in which the dream of authentic progress disseminated in Egyptian popular culture for most of the twentieth century was belied by the country's economic stagnation, as the heightened aspirations of the rapidly growing educated classes were crushed by the inability of the economy or the government to actualise the social mobility that schooling had promised. By the 1980s Egyptian movies, television shows and other popular culture forms had begun to question or even mock the importance of education, articulating the idea that 'something in the machinery of cultural transformation has gone drastically wrong',[20] creating a generation of young people for whom 'the official path of optimistic modernity is a distant rumour'.[21] The statistics have certainly been grim enough. In Cairo in the 1980s and 1990s, the employment rate showed an inverse correlation with educational attainment, so that the more education a person possessed, the more likely they were to be unemployed. While 80 per cent of the unemployed had at least a high school diploma, the unemployment rate for the uneducated was around 3 per cent. After a decade in the 1990s when the Egyptian economy was thrown into chaos by the expulsion of Egyptian workers from Kuwait after the Iraqi invasion, the 20 per cent inflation rate had calmed to about 5 per cent, but the unemployment rate still hovered around 10 per cent.[22] Far from being a specifically Egyptian phenomenon, the 'bitterly falsified hopes' of the educated in times of economic trouble have been a staple of official worries about the political implications of education in England, in India and elsewhere as well.[23] What matters is not necessarily the kind of education that is provided – training in medicine and engineering versus training in studio art or literature – but the common mismatch between the expectation of universal education and the fact that national economies often fail to provide employment opportunities for even the best-trained graduates.

Education as a Cultural System

> The charismatic hero ... acquires and retains (his authority) only by proving his powers in real life. He must perform miracles if he wants to be a prophet, acts of heroism if he wants to be a leader in war. Above all, however, his divine mission must 'prove' itself in that those who entrust themselves to him must prosper.[24]

For more than a century now, public discussion of education in the Middle East has been marked by two opposite idioms: that of hope and transformation, and that of crisis and failure. These idioms tend not to follow one another cyclically as new and improved educational programmes are implemented successfully and then become outmoded with time, the sort of growth-and-decay model Ibn Khaldun might have outlined had he worked for an education ministry. Instead, they persist in a state similar to what linguists call 'free variation', coexisting as binary alternatives, both expressing and generating nearly

constant anxiety and dissatisfaction with the current state of education, no matter what it looks like. The discourse of crisis and failure
accuses schools, along with the whole of the educational establishment,
of inefficiency, mismanagement, wilful disregard of the public good
and misdirection of effort. Schools are accused either of being hope-
lessly tradition-bound and out of step with the times; or, conversely,
of bending to every new fad and fashion, habitually failing to find
'what works' for students, for businesses, for sponsors, and for society
at large. In either case, schools never seem quite capable of providing
an appropriate body of knowledge and skills to their students (or their
'products', in the words of contemporary planners), or appropriate
'products' to the market.

The discourse of hope feeds on the discourse of failure by promising
that just one more set of modifications – training more science and
mathematics teachers, or providing more or less classroom time for
religion, or writing new history textbooks, or more emphasis on
music and art, or defunding music and art programmes in favour of
engineering and business management, or better assessment of student
learning, or regional quality assurance programmes, or more emphasis
on faculty research with better laboratories, or more emphasis on
student research and foreign study, or better critical thinking skills –
will create school graduates who can finally produce utopia: a society
without crime or unemployment, without immorality or fanaticism,
without hunger or fear. Moreover, proper schooling will create
both citizens and nations able to do something political leaders call
'competing in the knowledge-based global economy of the twenty-
first century'.

This theme of education as a competitive exercise on the part of
citizens rather than dynasties goes back to the turn of the last century.
By the 1860s, as Darwinian imagery began to suffuse public discussions
in Europe, social theorists like Gustave Le Bon, Herbert Spencer and
Edmond Demolins used the idea of competition to emphasise the role
of new, improved, modern educational systems in creating national
citizens able to adapt to the world's rapidly changing circumstances.

Not only were the educated to rise to the top of a rational social order within particular societies, but whole nations – forged by an education through which each individual would be able to overcome his purely local concerns and come to feel himself to be a member of the nation's collective soul – would compete with one another on a global scale.[25] In Egypt, Dr Alwi Pasha, the personal physician to King Fuad's sister, gave a speech in 1908 regarding the necessity of establishing a university in Egypt:

> Such is the law of civilization nowadays, requiring the mixing of nations, most of whom are the advanced nations, educated, civilized, and armed with weapons for the struggle of life (*al-jihad al-hayawi*). Do you want to remain unarmed until the natural law that the strong eat the weak is fulfilled? Hence everyone tells you: Learn. Be a man if you want to remain safe in this, the age of social struggle (*al-jihad al-ijtima'i*). And you can accomplish that only through (a) university ...[26]

The age of military struggle, in which Muhammad Ali, the Ottoman sultans or the Qajar Shah built educational capacity in order to fend off foreign military advances, had given way to 'the age of social struggle', thought of in terms not only of technological and military strength, but in Eurocentric terms of the adequacy of a country's civilisation or cultural and political development. As before, the newest higher education initiatives of the Middle Eastern states are growing not out of the cultural context of 'traditional' forms of education in the region,[27] but out of a struggle conceived in more purely economic terms and in the cultural context of a new set of standards defining international higher education practice itself.

This set of transnational practices is increasingly seen through the lens of the broader philosophical foundation of neo-liberalism, a world view which implies that catering to market forces and utilising the attendant management logics of efficiency and growth are the appropriate and even inevitable goals and standards for social, economic and political activity. As an example, standardised documents like mission and vision statements, first popularised in the 1980s by business and management consultants, are now the stock in trade of educational leaders as well. One can compare statements across national boundaries and find little difference in spirit or even wording between them. Compare, for example, a recent self-study project by the University of North Carolina system that can stand as a template for nearly any contemporary government's mission statement for its schools and universities:

> UNC should educate its students to be personally and professionally successful in the 21st century and, to do so, should enhance the global competitiveness of its institutions and their graduates ... equipping (students) with the tools they will need to adapt to the ever-changing world.[28]

Compare to this the wording of the mission statement of the Qatar Foundation:

> To foster centers of excellence which develop people's abilities through investments in human capital, innovative technology, state of the art facilities, and partnerships with elite organizations thus raising the competency of people and the quality of life.[29]

This internationalised vocabulary of contemporary educational management, which includes concepts like accountability, transparency, privatisation, quality control, branding, auditing, excellence and ranking by funding level or bibliometrics, has been commented upon by Norwegian anthropologist Ulf Hannerz,[30] who raises the twin issues of national and disciplinary difference. While in the past universities have been seen as 'pre-eminently national institutions, guardians of national culture and propagators of knowledge useful to the modern state', universities now are perceived more often as transnationally significant institutions subject to relatively generic management practices. 'The popular recent practice of concentrating research funding in large lump sums in the hope of creating instant "centres of excellence"', he writes, 'probably fits better with the research practices of some disciplines than others. Yet decisions on such matters seem not always to be preceded by much careful analysis, and are perhaps at times motivated by an impatient desire to climb quickly up the ranking lists.'[31] Universities as corporate bodies of faculty who decide the nature of the curriculum and of their own research programmes give way to universities as commercial corporations whose direction is set by management personnel who sometimes have no academic background at all, but who have well-defined rubrics for measuring 'quality' or 'success.'

Neither the processes nor the goals of education are simple, and they often work at cross purposes. I would argue, in fact, that these crossed purposes are central to the social and political attractiveness of educational programmes at all levels, from primary to tertiary and graduate levels. Education has become a charismatic hero in Weber's sense precisely because so many interest groups can find in it a gleam of hope. Political elites look to education as a means of strengthening military technology and building political loyalty; religious authorities see it as a platform for cultural transmission;[32] nascent and aspirational middle classes see it as the gateway to social mobility, while established middle classes use it as a means to keep their offspring from downward mobility; business leaders see it as a source for well-trained employees. Education promises simultaneously to maintain the values and symbols of cultural heritage and to create a population driving process of continuous change and transformation. It promises all things to all people.

But just as patriarchal and bureaucratic forms of authority have their weaknesses, so charismatic authority is vulnerable as well. Its first vulnerability is the inevitable failure of the charismatic hero to demonstrate perpetually the miracles upon which his reputation rests. In the case of Egypt during the last quarter of the twentieth century, for example, education's promises evaporated in an economic and political climate deadlocked by internal power struggles and uncontrollable geopolitical events. In contemporary Iraq and Palestine, as well, even those individuals who can make it through the nation's crippled universities find their prospects no better than anyone else's.

In a very different vein, in Iran, Lebanon and Afghanistan in the 1970s and 1980s, university campuses provided platforms for organising political movements that later pulled those countries apart. Patriarchal and bureaucratic power structures on both domestic and national levels which have alternately sponsored and resisted the development of modern European-style schooling in the Middle East, hoping to manage its revolutionary potential for their own ends, find that the new classes and organisational capacities of university students can be difficult to control. In the words of historian Roy Mottahedeh, 'If education is the rare child born of the shared enthusiasm of intellectuals and the regime, it was a child that in many ways defeated the hopes of both parents.'[33] As Egyptian viceroy Sa'id Pasha mused in the 1850s, 'Why open the people's eyes (through education)? They will only be more difficult to rule.'[34] Education can prove threatening even on the most local level; in rural Turkey men try to restrict women's access to local libraries lest they encounter in science books information about genetics and reproduction that might threaten the traditional authority of males.[35]

The social benefits of education bring with them the threat of instability and an increasing need to adjust social and economic rewards to the aspirations of new classes of people. The Gulf, as a mercantile region, is uniquely poised to benefit economically from the post-nationalist ideology of neo-liberalism. But whatever the ruling interests, nationalist or capitalist, the educational enterprise will be shaped by forces outside itself. No matter how vibrant the economy and how great the need for petroleum engineers, computer scientists, architects and bankers, there is a corresponding need for artists, writers, philosophers and social workers. The issue of language in university instruction, and its relationship to local populations and international networks, remains to be satisfactorily addressed. And what of the educational needs and aspirations of the Gulf's millions of guest workers from Pakistan and the Philippines, from Algeria, Egypt and Yemen? Are educational benefits going to be for the 'national' population only? How far can transnationalist and post-nationalist enterprises be pushed before they threaten important local constituencies, on the one hand, or begin to inconvenience a highly trained and mobile international faculty, on the other? What happens when faculty, staff or students begin to explore unionisation or political organisation? Will neo-liberal practices like educational assessment continue to be deployed for their own sake, as ritual acts of fealty to international convention, or will we find ways – the difficulties are as acute in the United States and Europe as they are in the Middle East – to use assessment and other management techniques in ways that actually improve the quality and significance of teaching and research?

Conclusion

> Going to Qur'anic school for me, and for all children, was like being taken to the slaughterhouse ... it had a meaning akin to death.[36]

If education's first vulnerability as a charismatic hero is the difficulty of continuously fulfilling promises to its multiple constituencies, its second vulnerability is the tendency of charisma to degenerate into bureaucracy. Real charisma, according to Weber, 'is always the offspring of unusual circumstances', whether external political and economic change, or internal spiritual change.[37] Things begin to change 'when the charismatic followers and disciples become ... marked out by special rights, then vassals, priests, public functionaries, party officials, officers, secretaries, editors and publicists, or else employees, teachers or other professional interest groups ... The charismatically ruled, on the other hand, usually become tax-paying "subjects"... or law-abiding "citizens".'[38] Charisma is overtaken by the interests of groups holding social power, in order to claim for themselves the legitimacy it confers.

The institutionalisation of charisma glimpsed in the boyhood recollection of Muhammad al-Akwa' – what could have greater charisma than the speech of God himself? But what could be less inspiring than learning that speech by rote, as a foreign language unconnected to daily life and childhood desires? – brings us to a final observation about the transformation of educational experience. Anthropologist Margaret Mead, comparing childhood socialisation among the Manus of New Guinea with education as it was practised in the United States at the same time, pointed out that the difference between the two societies had to do with

> the shift from the need for an individual to learn something which everyone agrees he would wish to know, to the will of some individual to teach something which it is not agreed that anyone has any desire to know. Such a shift in emphasis could come only with the breakdown of self contained and self respecting cultural homogeneity ... (and the focusing of) the attention of the group upon the desirability of *teaching* as over against the desirability of *learning*.[39]

Attention shifts from an individual's quest to find masters who can teach him self-evidently useful skills, to a system in which authorities seek out students – both adults and children – as the objects of self-conscious missionary effort. Education, she writes, 'then becomes a concern of those who teach rather than of those who learn',[40] and this provides the basis for the development of concern over the methods, techniques and organisation of education. It is here also, with the differential authority and status of teacher and taught, that 'using education as a way of changing status is introduced, and another new component of the educational idea develops. Here the emphasis is still upon the need to learn – on the one hand, in order to alter status and, on the other, to prevent the loss of status by failure to learn.'[41]

The irony of contemporary education in the neo-liberal or post-modern world system is that the connections between learning and status have shifted again. Classical standards of education like those faced by Muhammad al-Akwa', as little as he liked them at the time, delineated a set corpus of texts,[42] or more broadly, an idea about the ultimate intellectual or spiritual destination of an individual seeking knowledge. The model of the teacher, or ultimately the sense that people knew what appropriate and desirable knowledge was, provided guidance. One might not be able to know everything, but one at least knew in what direction to seek. In the view of contemporary educational establishments, with their emphasis on flexibility, knowledge creation, international competition and the ideology of 'life-long learning', those goals and models of ultimate knowledge have vanished. While classical educational theory viewed humans as potentially perfectible individuals pursuing a fixed, high goal of personal and spiritual development, neo-liberalism views them as productive units constantly to be trained and retrained to match the shifting needs of the global political economy. But *should* we be so busy establishing institutions that tell us there is no goal other than to chase the whims of the market? I think, in the end, that one of the most important questions we can ask about education in this new century – whether we live in Britain or Japan or Argentina or Kuwait – is whether this is really the kind of ideology we want to encourage, and really the kind of world we wish to build and to live in.

Notes

1. James Kay-Shuttleworth, 1870, quoted in Gregory Starrett, *Putting Islam to Work: education, politics and religious transformation in Egypt*, Berkeley 1998, p. 23.

2. Max Weber, 'The Nature of Charismatic Domination', in W. G. Runciman, ed., *Weber: selections in translation*, Cambridge 1978, p.233.

3. Ibid., p. 232.

4. Ibid.

5. Quoted in Bernard Lewis, *Islam: from the prophet Muhammad to the capture of Constantinople*, vol. II, *Religion and Society*, Oxford 1974, p. 280.

6. Ahmad Shalaby, *History of Muslim Education*, Beirut 1954, pp. 120–3.

7. Amira Nowaira, 'Lost and Found', in W. M. Hutchins, ed., *Egyptian Tales and Short Stories of the 1970s and 1980s*, Cairo 1987, pp. 109–12.

8. See, for example, Diego Gambetta and Steffen Hertog, 'Engineers of Jihad', Sociology Working Papers, no. 2007-10, Department of Sociology, University of Oxford, www.sociology.ox.ac.uk/research/workingpapers/2007-10.pdf.

9. Helen Lefkowitz Horowitz, *Campus Life: undergraduate cultures from the end of the eighteenth century to the present*, New York 1987, p. 4.

10. Benjamin C. Fortna, *Imperial Classroom: Islam, the state, and education in the late Ottoman empire*, Oxford 2000.

11. See also Monica M. Ringer, *Education, Religion, and the Discourse of Cultural Reform in Qajar Iran*, Costa Mesa, CA 2001.
12. Fortna, pp. 65–6.
13. Gertrude Bell, *Review of the Civil Administration of Mesopotamia*, London 1920, p. 11.
14. Ibid.
15. Starrett, *Putting Islam to Work*.
16. Mine Ener, *Managing Egypt's Poor and the Politics of Benevolence, 1800–1952*, Princeton 2003.
17. Jane Goodman, *Berber Culture on the World Stage: from village to video*, Bloomington 2005.
18. For the case of Egypt see Donald M. Reid, *Cairo University and the Making of Modern Egypt*, Cambridge 1990.
19. Walter Armbrust, *Mass Culture and Modernism in Egypt*, Cambridge 1996.
20. Ibid., p. 20.
21. Ibid., p. 146.
22. See Homa Hoodfar, *Between Marriage and the Market: intimate politics and survival in Cairo*, Berkeley 1997, and Armbrust, pp. 133–5.
23. Starrett, *Putting Islam to Work*, pp. 235–6.
24. Weber, p. 229.
25. Gregory Starrett, 'When Theory is Data: coming to terms with "culture" as a way of life', in Melissa J. Brown, ed., *Explaining Culture Scientifically*, Seattle 2008.
26. Quoted in Reid, pp. 31–2.
27. Jonathan P. Berkey, 'Madrasas Medieval and Modern: politics, education, and the problem of Muslim identity', in Robert W. Hefner and Muhammad Qasim Zaman, eds, *Schooling Islam: the culture and politics of modern Muslim education*, Princeton, 2006, pp. 40–60.
28. University of North Carolina Tomorrow Commission, *Final Report*. Chapel Hill, NC 2008.
29 www.qf.edu.qa.
30. Ulf Hannerz, 'The Neo-Liberal Culture Complex and Universities: a case for urgent anthropology?', in *Anthropology Today*, vol. 23, no. 5, pp. 1–2.
31. Ibid., p. 2.
32. Eleanor A. Doumato and Gregory Starrett, eds., *Teaching Islam: textbooks and religion in the Middle East*, Boulder 2007.
33. Roy Mottahedeh, *The Mantle of the Prophet: religion and politics in Iran*, Oxford 2000, p. 66.
34. Quoted in Starrett, *Putting Islam to Work*, p. 220.
35. Carol Delaney, *The Seed and the Soil: gender and cosmology in Turkish village society*, Berkeley 1991, p. 231.
36. Muhammad al-Akwa' (b. 1903), Yemeni teacher, political activist and *qadi*,

quoted in Brinkley Messick, *The Calligraphic State: textual domination and history in a Muslim society*, Berkeley 1993, p. 75.

37. Weber, p. 235.
38. Ibid., pp. 236–7.
39. Margaret Mead, 'Our Educational Emphases in Primitive Perspective', in *American Journal of Sociology*, vol. 48, no. 6, p. 634.
40. Ibid., p. 635.
41. Ibid.
42. See Messick and Berkey.

FIVE

Towards a Regional Quality Assurance Agency for the Middle East and Gulf Region

Moudi al-Humoud

Introduction

In this chapter I would like to raise some of the issues in higher and further education in the Middle East and Gulf Region and reflect on our path to the future. The main issue is how we can best safeguard the quality of higher education and be assured that academic provision and academic awards meet high standards and that they are responsive to our cultural values, traditions and the requirements of our expanding economies and social developments. To develop a policy for the future, we need to look beyond the shores of the Gulf and see how issues of this kind have been tackled in other countries. The lessons learnt from the British educational experience offer us a useful example.

Global Aspects of Higher Education

Over the last fifty years, we have witnessed fundamental changes in our world, such as advances in technology, the IT revolution, the advent of the Internet and the emergence of multinationals and interconnected economies. People can travel to distant lands at low cost, cultural interactions have increased and cross fertilised, and different cultures have sometimes clashed with each other. During these years, education at all levels has undergone profound changes: what was once the privilege of a few has become more accessible through widening access and innovative ideas such as open and distance learning. In addition to self-enlightenment, educational developments have provided increasingly knowledge-based economies with a highly educated workforce. Freer interaction between our nations has also internationalised our educational establishments: thousands of our younger generation go abroad for a better or different education, and an increasing number of Western universities have been opening branches in the Middle East, the Gulf and in other regions of the world. In Kuwait, for example, we have a state university (the University of Kuwait), authorised by the state to offer its own degree awards, and several other private universities affiliated with British, American and Australian institutions. Our own university, the Arab Open University, with campuses in seven Arab countries, is affiliated with the British Open University (OU-UK). We offer academic programmes based on Open University courses, and are accredited by the Open University Validation Services (OUVS) to offer OU-UK awards. Other private universities are allowed to operate on the basis of affiliation with an accredited and reputable parent institution, for example Dartmouth College, New Hampshire, USA, in the case of the American University of Kuwait.

Power to Offer Awards

Prior to 1992, British higher education was a binary system, comprising universities, with the power to offer degree awards, and polytechnics and colleges of further education with no such power. The latter institutions normally offered external degrees of London University or degrees through awarding bodies such as the Council for National Academic Awards (CNAA). The Higher and Further Education Act of 1992 changed this binary system and polytechnics were turned into universities, which were authorised to award degrees.

The CNAA was abolished and OUVS succeeded it, with a modified agenda. Similarly, all state universities in the Middle East and the Gulf Region are authorised to offer awards by state legislations, but other private universities and further education establishments must seek authorisation to offer internationally recognised degrees.

Quality Assurance

To chart the future of higher education, the UK government established the National Committee of Inquiry into Higher Education (NCIHE) in 1996, chaired by Sir Ron Dearing. His brief was 'To make recommendations on how the purposes, shape, structure, size and funding of higher education, including support for students, should develop to meet the needs of the United Kingdom over the next 20 years ...' The government asked the Committee to have regard, within the constraints of spending priorities and available budgets, to principles such as the following:

- 'the standards of degrees and other higher education qualifications should be at least maintained, and assured'
- 'value for money and cost-effectiveness should be obtained in the use of resources'
- 'maximum participation in higher education, provision of effectiveness of teaching and learning', and that
- 'learning should be increasingly responsive to employment needs and include the development of general skills, widely valued in employment'.[1]

A similar committee was set up to study the Scottish system of higher education, chaired by Sir Ron Garrick.

In their successive reports, Dearing and Garrick outlined a model for assuring quality and standards in UK higher education and proposed that the Quality Assurance Agency (QAA) should be given the task of managing its development and implementation. Since then, the QAA has offered such services by working with institutions and other stakeholders to provide public assurance of the quality and standards of higher education. A framework for qualifications, awards and benchmark standards across all subject areas has been developed. To assure quality, institutional systems for protecting the quality of academic provision and the standards of awards are reviewed, and the outcomes they achieve are measured against relevant standards and the objectives of each programme, and so on.[2] Thus, quality assurance, standards and benchmarks have become the yardstick for measuring the quality of higher education.

Quality Assurance Issues in the Middle East and Gulf Region

Now let us return to higher education in Kuwait and elsewhere in the Middle East and Gulf region. As remarked at the start, we need to develop a system for assuring the quality of our higher education, in order to ensure that our academic awards meet high standards and that we are responsive to the cultures and traditions of the region, the requirements of our expanding economies and social developments. Achieving this is facilitated by a widening consensus among educational authorities and institutions in the region that a 'regional quality assurance agency' should be established to monitor QA standards and accredit academic awards. Such an agency will develop subject benchmarks and standards by building on the variety of currently existing benchmarks and standards in the countries of the region, as well as those of similar agencies in other countries. In broad terms, it will assist institutions in enhancing the quality of their courses and academic programmes; promote public confidence in the region in the standards of awards; and provide reliable public information about the meaning of these awards for potential students, employers, governments and so on. Moreover, it will provide a measure of accountability for the financial resources of the institutions in the region.

A framework for qualifications will be established, defining awards, assisting the development of benchmarks for various subjects and providing the external examiners with a point of reference. Indeed, external examiners will play a pivotal role in the verification of the achievement of standards. In sum, the range of remits for the proposed

agency are similar to the ones put forward by the QAA in its response
to the Dearing and Garrick reports.[3]

Towards a Regional Quality Assurance Agency

The regional agency that has been briefly described can also be justi-
fied in terms of academic awards. At present, for example, in Kuwait
it is the national university which has the authority to award degrees
and, as mentioned above, private universities and colleges of further
education offer degrees of the parent institutions. Consequently,
there are a multitude of degrees which are sometimes difficult to
compare. This can be a problem for the graduates of these universities, as employers would like to be sure that their future employees
have attained certain minimum academic or technical standards. The
proposed regional quality assurance agency will establish a rational
and transparent basis for such comparisons.

It would be reasonable to expect some scepticism towards this idea
among academics and administrators in the institutions of the region.
Looking again at the British example, let us remind ourselves that the
British academics' initial response to the Dearing recommendations
was not entirely favourable: it was thought that they would encroach
on individual academic freedom; dent the independence of academic
institutions, some of which are centuries old; introduce redundancies
through the back door, etc. But more than a decade later, assurance
of quality has been recognised as a safeguard for academic excellence,
putting the interests of the students at the heart of the academic
enterprise. Similarly, we believe our institutions in the region will
respond to the establishment of the regional quality assurance agency
with, perhaps, some initial scepticism but that, once the benefits of
such an agency to the higher education systems in the region are
fully recognised, the academic establishments will participate in its
development and make it work for the benefit of all.

The Role of the Agency in Regional Development

The Middle East is recognised as one of the most sensitive geopolitical regions of the world, rich with oil and minerals that our economies and further development are dependent on. This region has a young population which strives for higher education. To preserve our standards of living and to continue the development of the region we have to expand our plans for investment in our people. In the sphere of education, this involves improving our system of education and widening educational opportunities for our younger generation, so that we can steadily move towards a more sustainable knowledge-based economy. The integrity of the regional higher education degree awards necessitates the establishment of a regional quality assurance agency responsible for periodic accreditation and validation of the institutions of higher education. In addition it will ensure that international quality assurance standards are adhered to, and will guide and monitor the development of higher education in the region.

Notes

1. R. Dearing, *The National Committee of Inquiry into Higher Education (Dearing Report)*, London 1997.
2. QAA, *Higher Quality 2* and *Higher Quality 3*, 1997; www.qaa.co.uk.
3. Ibid.

SIX

The Dilemma of Gender-Separated Higher Education in the United Arab Emirates

Jane Bristol-Rhys

The United Arab Emirates University opened in 1977 with 502 students divided between two gender-separated campuses. This marked the beginning of government-supported higher education in the United Arab Emirates. In 2008 there are indications that such perceptions about the necessity of gender-segregated higher education are changing. Indeed, as new institutions such as New York University, Yale, Paris-Sorbonne, George Mason and the New York Institute of Technology open mixed-gender campuses in the country and continue the trend started by the American University in Dubai, American University of Sharjah, 'Ajman University and Abu Dhabi University, it appears that only government-funded campuses will remain divided. Following a brief chronological summary of higher education in the UAE, this chapter identifies some problematic issues associated with gender-divided education and Emirati social norms that continue to resist integrating the sexes in the classroom. The perspectives expressed in this chapter reflect seven years of teaching Emirati women at Zayed University in Abu Dhabi, one of the country's gender-separated universities, and draw heavily on dialogues, debates and student opinions as we have discussed the changes that are affecting their society.

Higher Education in the UAE: a brief synopsis

The first federally funded university in the UAE was United Arab Emirates University (UAEU), which was located in Al-'Ayn.[1] Opened in 1977, UAEU now has over 13,000 students from all seven of the UAE's emirates.[2] Students from more distant emirates reside in dormitories during the week and are required to return home at the weekends. Both classrooms and dormitory residences are gender-separated. Females now represent over 70 per cent of the student body.[3] Faculty who teach at UAEU have male and female sections of the same class on different campuses. In response to the pressing need for training in technical and professional fields, the Higher Colleges of Technology (HCT) were established in 1988. The HCT system now operates twelve single-sex campuses throughout the country that serve over 16,000, students over 50 per cent of whom are female.[4] The HCT system has evolved over the years and now offers a more comprehensive curriculum that includes courses, programmes, certificates and diplomas of study in several applied fields. In 1998, after several years of consultation and curriculum design, Zayed University opened campuses in Abu Dhabi and Dubai. Zayed University, named after Shaikh Zayed bin Sultan Al Nahayan, the UAE's first president, was exclusively for Emirati women. Although graduate study in business, public administration, healthcare management and other programmes are now gender mixed, future expansion of university facilities will include separate campuses for men in both cities.[5]

The number of Emirati women actively pursuing higher education is significantly higher than their male counterparts who often opt for careers in the military, police or the petroleum industry, in which case they attend specialised training. Abu Dhabi's Petroleum Institute, one such specialised institution, now admits women as well. The UAE is a multi-cultured and, indeed, transnational society and as such is home, sometimes in the short term and sometimes for decades, to many nationalities. This transnationality is manifest in the number of private primary and secondary schools throughout the country that offer language and curriculum-specific education for Indian, German, American, Pakistani, British and Japanese pupils, and Arab pupils from other countries. If the plethora of private universities is any indication, then a significant number of high school graduates choose to stay in the UAE to pursue higher education as well. Indeed, there are now several institutions that serve the foreign community: the American University in Dubai, American University of Sharjah, 'Ajman University, Abu Dhabi University and George Mason University.[6] All of these campuses admit Emirati students as well, though they are usually outnumbered by the foreign students. In 2006 the Paris-Sorbonne Abu Dhabi opened, in 2007 the New York Institute of Technology; over the next few years New York University and Yale will follow suit.[7]

Inherent here are several intriguing issues in what appears to be the mushrooming of educational institutions, not the least of which is that education seems to be big business in the UAE. But for my focus the key point to be underscored is that all of these new institutions will be running their programmes on gender-mixed campuses. Similarly, the planned multi-university compound that will be known as Dubai Knowledge Universities will also integrate the sexes. Dubai's Knowledge Village, which opened its doors in 2003, now houses sixteen educational institutions that offer specialised study for both undergraduates and graduates in gender-mixed environments.[8] Knowledge Village resembles the educational version of free zones such as Jebel Ali which operates close by. Foreign educational institutions and programmes are able to lease space and set up operations quickly in a custom-built environment that substantially reduces the costs of opening a branch campus or an off-site programme.

The financial consequences of maintaining gender-separate higher education are not insignificant. The facilities and amenities necessary for a twenty-first-century campus, including telecommunications, laboratories, computers, sports equipment, cafeterias, recreational outlets and, in some locations, dormitories that must also be wired for the Internet, are a substantial investment. Constructing and then maintaining duplicate campuses to segregate the sexes adds significantly to what is already an expensive proposition. It is not the case that two replica campuses represent an equal investment to one single campus with the capacity to serve the combined number of students. Two campuses inevitably cost more and any economies of scale are lost. A large chemistry laboratory accommodating a class of thirty is cheaper to build and maintain than two laboratories in two different sites for fifteen students each.[9] The costs involved in maintaining separate campuses is perhaps one motivation behind the trend to move away from gender-separated learning in non-government-funded higher education. Indeed, even institutions such as Abu Dhabi University and Al-Hosn University that are supported by prominent Abu Dhabi families now have gender-integrated campuses (although the actual classes are conducted separately).[10]

The rapid proliferation of private institutions of higher education in the UAE might appear to suggest that the government is gradually reducing its involvement. However, this is not the case and the expansion of UAEU's Al-'Ayn campus, the new Dubai campus for Zayed University, the new Abu Dhabi women's campus for HCT and the proposed new Abu Dhabi campus for Zayed University indicate that the UAE government remains firmly committed to higher education and more specifically to gender-separated education.[11]

Problematic Issues

Cost might appear to be a trivial issue when discussing the system of higher education in a wealthy country such as the UAE. But we must note that UAE citizens are educated entirely free of charge. Emirati students pay no tuition fees and they receive their textbooks and science and art supplies free of charge.[12] In the case of Zayed University, students must purchase a laptop computer to support their studies but other than that – and buying notebooks, pens and lunch in the cafeteria – there are no expenses. The federal budget for all grades of education was 7.1 billion dirhams in 2007. The 2008 budget for higher education is 2.3 billion dirhams.[13]

Given greater female attendance rates at UAEU, and at HCTs throughout the country, as well as the all-female Zayed University campuses, it appears that most of the money is being spent on women's higher education.[14] This is now reflected in the job market as well. Emirati women are participating in the labour force at appreciably greater rates. The rate has grown by almost 10 per cent in the years between 1995 and 2004.[15] While this rate is low in comparison with data from countries in the industrialised West, it is a notable and significant change in the UAE. As the nation's official yearbook points out, 'UAE society is patriarchal and the changing of traditional views concerning women's place in the family is a slow process.'[16] Traditional views such as these undoubtedly continue to shape women's education. There are a considerable number of families who, while now supporting the idea of college or university study for their daughters, would never concede to allowing their daughters to attend a gender-integrated campus or class.[17] Indeed, the security arrangements on women's campuses are stringent. All visitors, and most especially males, must be vetted, signed in and appropriately tagged before entering any part of the campus. Security measures extend to the students as well. At Zayed University a student may not leave the campus at any time without the approval of her parents or, in the case of married students, her husband. Once on campus a student is prohibited from leaving between classes unless she has secured, with written approval, a green card pass. My students jokingly refer to the university campus as the Abu Dhabi women's prison and while a few breakouts have occurred over the years, they have been motivated more by the dire need for ice cream or a shopping expedition than anything more sinister. The security measures put in place on the women's campuses are an assurance given to parents that their daughters will be safe and, perhaps more importantly, be seen to be safe. Emirati society has experienced enormous changes over the past forty years, but it is still very much regulated by traditional social norms that prohibit social interaction between extra-familial males and females. The social control exerted by such norms is perhaps heightened by the fact that Emiratis are highly visible in national dress: given the small size of the Emirati community, it is often the case that people recognise each other or at the very least know the family, however distantly.

In the pre-oil era, women worked hard. In the shaikhdom of Abu Dhabi the household economies of many families were in the hands of the women. Women were responsible for the date harvest in the oases because the majority of the men would be diving in the waters of the Gulf during the pearling season. Most women lived their lives surrounded by family, first in their natal families and then in their affinal families. In most cases these two categories were one and the same, reflecting the cultural preference for *bint 'am* (first cousin) marriages. My focus here precludes a full discussion of women's status and the cultural notions of family and honour in Gulf Arab society, but it is noteworthy to consider that many of the older Emirati women I have interviewed insist that they had much more contact with extra-familial males in their youth than the current generation of Emirati females. They shopped in the markets, negotiated with traders and conducted business with the members of other tribal groupings. One Emirati woman, now in her late seventies, recounted how she contracted men of another tribe to gather wood for her family's charcoal business. She had no reservations about dealing face to face with the men as long as she was wearing her *burqah* (face cover), but today she wouldn't think of even saying hello to a man in public.[18] With wealth, Emirati society changed and women withdrew from many public activities as their economic role was erased. From my discussions with students, their mothers and their grandmothers, it appears that it is the generation of women born in the 1960s who experienced the greatest tightening of social norms. These women, now in their late forties and early fifties, did go to high school but perceived few opportunities to continue their studies or carry out any work outside of the family once they were married. Their daughters are my students and for this younger generation there is now considerable pressure being brought to bear by the government for them to work and have productive careers in addition to raising families.

The nation's efforts to reduce dependence on the foreign workforce would seem to be the cause of this pressure. Expatriates outnumber Emiratis by an estimated ratio of 8 to 1, while their presence in the workforce is even more distorted. According to official reports:

> At present the majority of the national workforce, 88 per cent, is working in a public sector that has reached saturation point and is, therefore, incapable of absorbing the 16,187 nationals entering the job market in 2006. This figure will rise to 19,610 in 2010 and 40,000 by 2020. At present, UAE nationals account for a very small percentage of the total workforce in the private sector, while private sector employment accounts for 52.1 per cent of the jobs in the UAE. [19]

'Emiratisation' is the government's policy to encourage and in some places insist upon the employment of Emiratis.[20] For several years the banking industry has been implementing a mandatory 15 per cent rate of employment of Emiratis and now other sectors of the economy, including human resources and public affairs, are to be staffed exclusively by Emiratis.[21] In 2004 over 66 per cent of Emirati job seekers were women, and that percentage continues to increase, along with the number of women in institutions of higher education.[22]

As more Emirati women join the workforce, they will necessarily have to interact with more men. This eventuality looms large because there are fewer and fewer jobs to be found in what were once called 'women-only environments'. A women-only environment was not a workplace devoid of all men, just one characterised by the absence of Emirati men. Foreign males, whether corporate executives or office cleaners (European, North American, Indian or Arab), do not figure in the equation. Similarly, women's universities, campuses and classrooms do not imply an absence of male faculty, just an absence of Emirati men of the same age group as the students.

This is possibly the most potentially dysfunctional aspect of gender-segregated higher education in the UAE. Women who have attended all-female institutions are expected and encouraged to become active participants in the workforce and yet they have no experience of interacting with men and have been systematically prevented from doing so. Indeed, even the prospect of close proximity can prove to be both exciting and daunting. The masters programmes offered by Zayed University are all gender mixed and this has brought Emirati men to the campus. The men are restricted to the one building in which their class is held but that building also houses the library and so female students can see the men and be seen by them. Quite a few students became agitated when the men appeared and they quickly moved to the inner core of the campus, away from the men. Many seemed to find the situation an amusing novelty and they stared unabashedly at the men whenever they were out of their classroom. Six of my students arrived late for class, announcing that 'there were men on campus'. The presence of Emirati men on the campus has gradually lost the lustre of excitement and the students respond to their presence now by simply re-wrapping their *shaylah* (headscarf) a little more tightly.

An internship period is currently required of all students at Zayed University, as is the case at many other universities in the UAE. This ten-week period often represents the first time that most students will be in an environment that is not strictly controlled and one in which they must interact with Emirati men. The amount of interaction varies according to the internship site but for the last several years all of the students I have placed and supervised in internship – around fifty – worked with at least two Emirati men. Many of that number had male supervisors and some were involved in projects that required working alongside and directly with Emirati men. The students' initial verbal reaction to this imminent scenario was 'I can't' and nearly all were quite terrified at the idea of working with an Emirati man. What to say, how to act and how not to act were and are just some of their concerns. Happily most adjust rapidly and then express amazement at how frightened they were at the outset. One problem is, however, very difficult for the women to overcome. That is the belief that they cannot or should not assert their opinion on an issue even when fully convinced that the man is incorrect. 'I can't tell a man that he is wrong' replied one student when I asked her how and why her joint research project had gone so far astray. Another student sat back and allowed her male counterpart to mangle an English translation because she felt she 'couldn't show him up'. A few years ago one of my interns argued stridently with her Lebanese male supervisor but would not intervene when the Emirati man with whom she was working wreaked havoc on the database she was building. I was incredulous and confronted her on this double standard. She informed me that there had to be a double standard because if she challenged her Emirati co-worker he would have had his pride injured and he might retaliate by spreading rumours about her or, in her words, blacken her name. When I pointed out that the quality of the work she was doing should come first in her mind, I was reminded that Emirati society is patriarchal and that the men do not seek the opinion of women nor do they encourage women to have opinions, much less express them. While I was certainly gratified that this student had absorbed much in her anthropology classes, this exchange drew my attention to one problem inherent in gender-separated higher education in the Emirates; we are not teaching women, or men for that matter, how to work together.

I have pursued this idea with my students in class discussions on subjects ranging from Emiratisation to the changing public role of women, and we have also discussed the perceived obstacles that might prevent women from building careers and the social norms of Emirati society. Over my fourteen semesters and many hundreds of classes, the students have remained consistent in their expressed opinion that much more needs to change in Emirati society before women will be taken seriously in the workforce, or anywhere else. While government media sources often showcase the achievements of Shaikha Lubna Al Qasimi, the new Minister of Foreign Trade, my students point out that she is from the ruling family of Sharjah and a protégé of the ruler of Dubai and that the combination of those two factors make her much less of a real-life role model than press releases would have us believe. Somewhat closer to reality is the model presented by Shaikha Fatima Al Qitbi, the wife of the late Shaikh Zayed. She is often referred to as 'the mother of the nation' and her work encompasses women's rights, women's welfare and countless other philanthropic projects. Significantly, she is never photographed and never appears in public when men are present. She is a quiet force and stays behind the scenes in a manner fitting the public and private spheres of influence in the Arab world.[23] For my students Shaikha Fatima is therefore a much more accessible role model. She is conservative, hidden from the public view, does not compete with men in any arena and works to promote women from within the system. Shaikha Fatima does indeed set the tone for the roles assumed by other female members of the ruling family in Abu Dhabi. Rarely does one see a shaikha's name in the paper unless it is to recognise the support given to a particular cause or an event. It was rather startling to see the name of Shaikha bint Saif, the wife of Shaikh Sultan bin Khalifa Al Nahayan, mentioned in the online version of *Gulf News* recently and, perhaps more striking, that it was reported that she had opened a bridal exhibition in person. Apparently I was not the only person to be rather shocked by this because when I returned to the site four hours later her name and her presence at the opening had both been excised from the article.

This may well be the dilemma that faces Emirati women in the years to come. Government policies that encourage women to study and to work are in essence top-down directed social changes that may be proceeding at a pace too fast for many families. University-aged Emirati women are caught somewhere in the middle of this and quite openly verbalise the pressure they feel. Sadly, some of the brightest and the best will never be able to contribute because they will not be permitted to work. One of these, a recent internship student, pleaded with me to extend her time as an intern because she knew that this was her only chance to experience working as her father would not permit her to have a job. Other students have watched their dreams of graduate studies evaporate before their eyes as fathers have intervened. Emirati women will be exceedingly well educated, more so than their husbands in some cases, yet the majority will shy away from public roles and publicity. When I ask students what they think about marrying someone who is less educated, they shrug their shoulders and smile. 'We may have to become stupid again,' they say, but then they quickly add, 'but our daughters will never have to, we will see to that'.

Notes

1. Higher Education in the UAE is funded and regulated by the Ministry of Higher Education and Scientific Research. The Ministry approves the budgets for all public sector universities.

2. L. U. Soffan, *The Women of the United Arab Emirates,* London 1980, p. 57.

3. *United Arab Emirates Yearbook,* Dubai 2007, p. 238.

4. See the HCT website: www.hct.ac.ae/flash/factsNfigures/facts.html?p=hct.

5. See the Zayed University website: www.zu.ac.ae.

6. This is not a comprehensive listing. There are also discipline-specific joint educational ventures such as the Dubai School of Government/Georgetown University, as well as a myriad of institutes for technological training, computer training and so forth.

7. Jane Bristol-Rhys, 'Internal Report on Zayed University/Yale Joint Meetings', Abu Dhabi 2007.

8. For a detailed list of these institutions see www.kv.ae.

9. Jane Bristol-Rhys, 'Bin Brook Construction Interview', Abu Dhabi 2007.

10. It is difficult at times to draw a clear distinction between government and prominent families as the latter dominate the former. Institutionalised patronage requires that a high-ranking shaikh or shaikha gives sponsorship to new ventures and it is not always clear if that patronage includes financial support. Al-Hosn University is very clearly funded by Abu Dhabi Holdings but exactly who is represented in that corporation is less clear. See www.adh.ae.

11. *United Arab Emirates Yearbook 2007,* pp. 232–3.

12. Soffan, p. 57.

13. See www.uaeinteract.com/docs/Cabinet_approves_biggest_zero-deficit_budget_/27669.htm.

14. *United Arab Emirates Yearbook 2007,* p. 238.

15. Tanmia, 'Human Resources Report 2005', Dubai 2005.

16. *United Arab Emirates Yearbook 2007,* p. 243.

17. Soffan, p. 54.
18. Jane Bristol-Rhys, 'Emirati Grandmothers', field interviews in Al 'Ayn, 2006.
19. *United Arab Emirates Yearbook 2007*, p. 217.
20. Christopher M. Davidson, *The United Arab Emirates: a study in survival*, London 2005, pp. 145–54.
21. *United Arab Emirates Yearbook 2007*, pp. 218–19.
22. Ibid., p. 238.
23. C. Nelson, 'Public and Private Politics: women in the Middle Eastern world', in *American Ethnologist*, vol. 1, no. 3, pp. 551–63.

SEVEN

The United Arab Emirates and Policy Priorities for Higher Education

Warren H. Fox

Building for the future and providing access to higher education for Emiratis and expatriates is fast becoming a policy priority for the United Arab Emirates. The future relationship between public higher education institutions and the economy is, however, different in the UAE from most other countries due to its massive oil wealth, and also the extraordinary extent of its economic diversification, its rapidly expanding workforce and the enormous social upheavals that are taking place in the country.

Since 2002, the price of oil has quadrupled, and the revenues of the Gulf Arab states 'are likely to be near last year's record $336 billion, giving them an edge in buying foreign assets'.[1] Further, *The Economist* reported on a 'multi-billion-dollar windfall' for Gulf states as the price of oil went past $60 per barrel. It chronicled record levels of income, and in turn record levels of investment in the six Gulf Cooperation Council countries.[2] Another report predicted that revenue increases 'might be in the region of 50 to 100 billion dollars over the next decade'.[3] This wealth allows the UAE to channel funds into foreign assets, but also into domestic areas, property development, construction, the stock market, banking, shipping and other areas of the expanding economy. Diversifying and developing the economy of the UAE have become national goals.

As the UAE pursues the development of these new economic sectors, it must also consider the workforce needed to enable such expansion. The UAE is very successful at importing expatriate-sector talent, as most of the employees in the private sector are from other countries. A key policy and strategic issue for the future is the ability to educate and train Emiratis for positions of leadership, ownership and staffing in their country's new economy. The colleges and universities operated by the federal government – the United Arab Emirates University, Zayed University and the Higher Colleges of Technology – are the foundation for the enrolment of Emiratis and their preparation for employment. Over 34,000 Emirati students are enrolled at no cost to themselves in programmes from the diploma level to the 'baccalaureate' degree,* and graduate programmes are also available with free tuition. However, building and maintaining the capacity of these institutions to enrol all national students in quality programmes have become a challenge for the future. Key policy choices need to be made to increase the capacity of tertiary education and improve social and economic benefits for the country. Although oil revenues are high, national investment in public sector higher education has not kept pace with fiscal needs.

Higher Education Policy

The UAE is rapidly developing into a regional and global model for economic and social development and higher education's ability to contribute is critical. The UAE, since the establishment of the United Arab Emirates University in Al-'Ayn in 1976, has made outstanding progress in higher education, expanding possibilities for Emiratis and providing quality programmes. The federal higher education campuses are positioned to build on their accomplishments for the

---

* Interestingly, in the UAE, bachelor degrees are always incorrectly referred to as baccalaureate degrees.

future depending upon federal fiscal and policy decisions. As Emiratis comprise approximately 20 per cent of the total population of over 4 million, it is imperative that UAE citizens attain high levels of education in order to provide leadership for the country's future and a talented workforce for its growing economy. Higher education can increase employment opportunities for success for men and women and serve national progress.

UAE leaders from both the public and private sectors expect national colleges and universities to strengthen, diversify and support the country's economic development. Because of rapid change in the region, the future success of the UAE depends upon an educated workforce and a high-quality higher education system. However, a crisis in funding exists and investment in the Higher Colleges of Technology, Zayed University and the United Arab Emirates University is urgently needed. To retain and achieve quality programmes for the UAE's development – a key strategic goal – funding must be increased. Current appropriations per student have fallen well below international standards.

Internationally, the forces of globalisation are creating an environment which demands that UAE citizens possess a wide array of new skills in order to function effectively in the new millennium. These forces are impacting all facets of education in the UAE, placing heavier demands on students, straining existing facilities and underscoring the need for society to have a sustained and expanded commitment to education. In late 2003 Shaikh Nahayan bin Mubarak Al Nahayan, the Minister of Higher Education and Scientific Research, recognised this issue and initiated a special national-level planning group aimed at advancing national educational policy in the UAE. This new planning group recommended the creation of a steering committee to guide what was envisioned as a very broad and sustained effort at reviewing national education policy. In March 2004 the steering committee issued a report entitled *Higher Education and the Future of the UAE* which addressed the most urgent areas of inquiry that the committee had reviewed. The report presented a series of findings and recommendations that related to higher education policy. These served as the impetus for the current comprehensive plan for higher education in the UAE.

In particular, the report noted that there were no federal policies or practices requiring broad coordination of missions, degrees, organisations or programmes between or among federal institutions. 'While there is coordination of application processes ... there is no coordination function or position at the ministry for the federal institutions.'[4] It recommended the creation of federal policy, as decisions were campus based and unrelated to each other. These and other considerations led the committee to recommend the creation of an Office of Higher Education Policy and Planning for federal institutions within the ministry. The office was established in mid-2004 to provide the effective coordination of education policy and the development of long-range plans to improve the capacity of the ministry and to implement policies that met the changing needs of the UAE. The challenge, however, given the stratified nature of political leadership and the traditions of the federal campuses, is to sustain and integrate a system-wide view of policy decisions. Traditional social relationships are strong and influential, data for decisions are often lacking and collaboration is only now beginning.

Responding to this need, the policy office led the development of the strategic plan of the ministry, entitled *Educating the Next Generation of Emiratis: a master plan for UAE higher education*, which was published in 2007. This clearly delineated the national goals as being: first, to provide access and educational opportunities for all Emiratis; second, to provide high-quality education; and third, to contribute to the UAE's economic development. The latter goal stated that: 'The academic programs and research efforts of the UAE system of higher education shall better link the national needs of the economy, prepare Emiratis for participation in the private sector, and expand leadership in energy production and economic development research.'[5] The achievement of this goal is critical to raise the number of Emiratis employed in the private sector and to support and expand their impact on growth.

Key Issues for Higher Education in the UAE

As outlined in the strategic plan, four key historic decisions were made in the 1970s in the UAE that shaped the character and structure of higher education in the country. These policies honour the values and practices of an Arab nation but also recognise modern demands of international education. They also had a major impact on the fiscal needs of public-sector higher education that persist to this day. There are four original pillars of policy for the UAE: the federal government would build and operate its own universities, separated by gender; a qualified, mostly international faculty would be employed; all instruction would be in English; and education was to be for all qualified Emiratis, and would include women.[6]

These key decisions were the pillars upon which federal higher education was established and they continue to serve the nation. They contribute to higher costs than other countries because importing faculty has higher fixed costs of providing housing and transportation home each year, and separating campus facilities by gender increases both capital costs and the number of faculty, but they also contribute to broad access and quality instruction. They are, moreover, policy choices that are based on cultural values and social expectations of the country. It is legitimate for a country with fiscal resources to support such policy choices if it chooses to do so.

Strategic Fundamentals: funding and access for UAE citizens

The number of Emiratis is increasing and more UAE citizens have recognised the importance of education, factors that have led to a steady increase in the number of applicants for admission to federal higher education institutions in the UAE. Enrolment is expected to increase by approximately 10,000 students over the next ten years, and by 20,000 by 2020.[7] The consequences of this trend were noted by the Advisory Committee for Planning of Higher Education in the United Arab Emirates a decade ago. The committee observed that there was a crisis in higher education because of chronic underfunding and the projected increases in student enrolment. These concerns now appear to have been well founded. Data developed by the Ministry of Higher Education's Office of Higher Education Policy and Planning suggest that the capacity of the higher education system to provide access to all qualified students has not only been reached, but exceeded. This was published in a report, *Funding Students First: access to quality higher education programs in the United Arab Emirates.*[8]

As is the case in any country, the adequacy of support for higher education depends upon two key factors: enrolment and inflation. As enrolment increases, the revenue per student declines without commensurate increases in financial support. Similarly, the 'real' value of static revenue – even with unchanging enrolment – would usually drop over time as the actual purchasing power of revenue declines. Table 7.1 estimates the purchasing power of funds allocated by the UAE Ministry of Finance to the country's three federal institutions of higher education. Enrolment from 2000 to 2006 grew by approximately 16 per cent across the UAE. By comparison, the real revenue declined by an estimated 14 per cent. Together, enrolment and inflation conspired to decrease the real value of federal support per student, which declined by over one-quarter between 2001 and 2006.

Table 7.1. Estimated Value of Support for UAE Federal Institutions

Year	2001	2002	2003	2004	2005	2006
Revenue from Ministry of Finance (Millions of AED)	1,411.9	1,476.4	1,492.3	1,511.0	1,517.0	1,541.1
Real revenue* (2001)	1,411.9	1,406.1	1,353.6	1,305.3	1,248.0	1,207.5
Enrolment (previous autumn)	29,670	31,430	33,384	33,498	34,207	34,336
Real revenue/ student	47,587	44,736	40,545	38,965	36,485	35,167

* Real revenue deflates funding using a simple 5 per cent estimate
Source: Institutional reports and Ministry of Higher Education and Scientific Research

This funding situation is leading to less than desirable outcomes for access and quality for UAE students. Per student expenditures as a percentage of GDP are low compared with other countries. This lack of funding results in students being turned away or being placed in institutions that do not have adequate funds to meet their needs. In order to be competitive with other countries and to achieve international standards, an increase to a level of over 3.5 per cent in GDP funding for higher education should occur in the UAE.[9]

Economic and GDP growth have been substantial in the UAE over the last several years. Since 2000, nominal GDP for the UAE has more than doubled by 2006. However, over the same time period higher education funding has been comparatively flat. Clearly the capacity for higher levels of support exists, though policy decisions have not been made for fiscal reasons. If allowed to continue, the present situation is likely to have significant consequences for UAE society. Frustrated students, unable to meet their educational goals, may opt for other activities that will either misuse or under-use their capacities. Students who do not have the chance to achieve their potential in the higher educational system are likely to be marginalised in the increasingly global and sophisticated economy that is now characteristic of the UAE.

The UAE needs to be committed to maintaining high-quality programmes, at Zayed University, United Arab Emirates University and the Higher Colleges of Technology, otherwise students and the country will not benefit from higher education, and top students will migrate to competitive institutions. There are many measures of quality in higher education. Among the more important of these are well-prepared student applicants, adequate funding, highly qualified faculty, modern facilities, state-of-the-art information technology, accreditation by external agencies and preparedness of graduates for the job market.

If graduates of UAE institutions of higher education are to compete successfully in the global marketplace for jobs in the private sector, the above measures of quality must be present. High-quality institutions of higher education are central to the UAE becoming more self-sufficient and to increasing the attractiveness of UAE graduates to private industry.

In addition to sufficient funding adequately to support the approximately 20,000 additional students that are anticipated up to the year 2020, it will also be necessary to support the quality of education the students receive.[10] In an important policy development, and in recognition of the funding issue for public-sector higher education, in early 2007 the Ministry of Presidential Affairs commissioned a study of the financing of federal institutions. This is an indication of awareness by policymakers of fiscal shortfalls that primarily affect access of Emirati students and programme quality. The study explored enrolment trends and Ministry of Finance and Industry appropriations over time. Funding alternatives are being considered, including a possible funding formula based on the number of students, although final recommendations are not yet available. However, there are possibilities that improved funding levels could be achieved, most likely with increased accountability and reporting requirements on budgeting and student outcomes. The federal government is demonstrating interest in improved data on institutional performance, student information, accountability and planning.

Federalism and Emirate-level Programmes

Profound changes are shaping higher education. At another government level, the emirate-level authorities are increasingly active in tertiary education, especially in the emirates of Dubai, Sharjah and Abu Dhabi. The UAE is a federation of seven emirates, formed in 1971. Nation building and federal activities have continued since then in all sectors, including education. In 1996 the Ministry of Higher Education and Scientific Research was established to deal with all federal educational institutions. It also provides admissions services through the National Admissions and Placement Office (NAPO), licenses private institutions and is responsible for the scholarship programme for Emiratis.

The Ministry of Education for primary and secondary education is far larger, overseeing ten educational zones and 700 schools. The decades-old trend of federal capacity building has now been affected by emirate-based units and organisations interested in local issues, specialised programmes and local control. Dubai, for example, established the Dubai Education Council in 2005 to address school reform, and created Knowledge Village as a free zone for higher education campuses. Abu Dhabi created the Abu Dhabi Education Council which is dealing with the emirate's educational priorities. The emirate of Sharjah has created community colleges and independent universities including the American University of Sharjah.

Dubai, ahead of other emirates, has designed future growth through a strategic plan, *The Dubai Strategic Plan 2015*, and is now establishing units of the Dubai government to oversee and implement goals. In April of 2007 Dubai created the Knowledge and Human Development Authority, headed by Abdulla al-Karam, to plan, coordinate and implement educational and training programmes for Dubai residents from early childhood through adult education – a lifelong approach to development. The government of Dubai has decided to offer non-federal and private-sector options in higher education through colleges and universities setting up in the free zones in Knowledge Village and the newer Academic City, and is considering expansion of government-sponsored institutions to increase access and quality as well as attracting first-rate international universities to open branches in Dubai – such as Michigan State University.

High potential exists for these entities to have major influence on higher education decisions and policy within their jurisdiction. Already emirates have begun programmes on school reform, school management and teacher education, and have established colleges and universities or entered into agreements with private providers. However, there has not been effective collaboration between these organisations, nor any joint planning. As these policy units are relatively new, their long-term impact is yet to be determined, but it is clear that local emirate initiatives and policies will have a significant impact upon the future of higher education in the UAE, and may lead to policy development and programme offerings in the country. The situation results in a more crowded policy environment and makes national policy more difficult to plan and implement. The situation may, however, result in increased choices for students to attend higher education programmes.

Quality of Education and College Readiness

The quality of education is critical to the future of the UAE. Quality overlaps all the other issues relating to higher education in the UAE. A system that does not meet internationally accepted standards of quality – in its staffing, in its programmes, in instructional technology and in its graduates – will not serve society well. Failure to maintain standards in all of these areas means that the job market will not welcome degree holders as readily, and this will in turn lead to students making other choices about their education. In order to certify quality, both the United Arab Emirates University and Zayed University are exploring comprehensive accreditation from a United States regional accrediting body, and are already receiving accreditation for specialised programmes such as engineering and education. At the emirate level, Dubai is considering a quality-assurance process for institutions in its jurisdiction.

The ministry's report on *Higher Education and the Future of the UAE* noted that only 5 per cent of those employed in the private sector are Emirati graduates. As the report notes, the data are not sufficient to confirm this situation fully, but such a seemingly low participation rate in the private sector is nevertheless a cause for concern. This is particularly true if the low participation rate is in part attributable to private-sector estimations of the educational achievements of UAE higher-education graduates.[11]

While the qualifications of graduates are important to the success of the UAE's higher education system, another important factor that must be considered is the capacity of students to complete what should be a demanding curriculum successfully. This depends in large part on the extent to which incoming students have been provided with the skills to learn at the university level. It is clear that a large number of students are not ready to work at the college level. Scores on the CEPA (Common Educational Proficiency Assessment) test show that far too many students do not have the necessary competencies in English to undertake college-level work. The scores are a strong predictor of success and every effort must be made to provide students with the tools needed for a successful higher education experience. At the same time, the resources that are now being spent on remedial courses in an effort to bring a large number of students up to an acceptable level in English are diverting funds and attention from the core mission of a university. A strategic advantage will emerge when there is a lower demand for such 'readiness' programmes.

Continued support for information technology (IT) is also central to the effective delivery of instruction, the storage and retrieval of information, and the conducting of research. Computers and IT have revolutionised higher education, and the capacity to utilise technology is therefore critical for UAE campuses. The federal institutions have set examples for the use of computer technology in improving learning, and through computers in instruction, networking, web-based resources and the use of laptops. The potential for further collaboration efforts among the campuses for digital libraries, learning centres and 'smart', IT-enabled classrooms is high. Technology contributes to innovation in teaching and learning and library services. Improving student skills in computer technology and the use of IT should therefore be a high priority for higher education.

Expand the Participation of Males in Higher Education

Of the many policy issues that are confronting the higher education system in the UAE, the percentage of male students enrolled in higher education (about 28 per cent) is one of the most troubling. There are many reasons for this low level of male enrolment in the higher education system, and correcting the problem will require policy initiatives that will demand significant resources and require a cooperative effort from many institutions in the

UAE. Before initiating major policy changes, the dimensions of the problem and its causes must be carefully assessed.

Data developed by the Institutional Planning Unit and the Admission and Registration Department of United Arab Emirates University indicate that male enrolment has lagged far behind female enrolment for the past twenty years. A 2004 survey by the National Admissions and Placement Office (NAPO) showed that 'over half of the male students (current school leavers) who had been approved for admission in September 2003 did not show up for registration.'[12] Interviews conducted during the development of this report suggested that there were many reasons for this low rate of male enrolment: young males have more opportunities available to them including joining the military, the police, participating in a family or other business, or working in some capacity for the government. Other observers expressed the view that young men perceive that it takes a long time to complete a higher education programme. The requirement to have demonstrated competency in English has acted as a deterrent, because at least a year must be spent getting to a level that will allow college-level work. The academic progress requirements were also identified as a possible hindrance to male enrolment.

Improving Tertiary Relationships with the Private Sector

Major efforts must be undertaken to increase the low percentage of nationals employed by the private sector. UAE citizens have become more aware of the value of education and increasingly understand the importance that education has in economic life. A very strong motivation for pursuing higher education is the prospect of lifelong economic benefits that accompany higher education. The higher education system of the UAE, like educational systems elsewhere, must have a close and durable relationship with the economic life of the country. The effort to establish and maintain relationships with the private sector has become part of the daily activity of UAE educational institutions. The long-term success of these institutions depends on the acceptance of its graduates by private organisations which value them for the skills and knowledge they have acquired through participating in the higher education system. Referring to a report by the International Labour Organisation, one author observed that the report 'insists that training and education were at the heart of Southeast Asia's economic miracle and could well provide a way out of under-development and poverty for millions of workers'.[13]

To serve as competent members of the UAE workforce, workplace skills are required of UAE nationals. Programme graduates from the diploma level to graduate degrees should possess the skills needed to be a productive member of an organisation. In addition to the attributes gained from a programme of study or an academic major, a workforce curriculum should be expanded within general education and major courses in campus offerings. In addition to producing graduates who can participate in the economy, the UAE also must continue to expand its capacity to serve the private sector's need for technical assistance and applied research. All components of the higher education system have established programmes of cooperative and applied research. The effort of the Centre for Externally Funded Research and Consultancy of United Arab Emirates University is one example of this activity and the Centre of Excellence for Applied Research and Technology at the HCT and the Institute for Applied Research at Zayed University are others. However, what is lacking is a clear list of national priorities for research and a competitive funding programme with federal funding at international levels. The master plan for UAE Higher Education contains a proposal for such a programme.

Non-federal Institutions and a Comprehensive Education Policy

The UAE's economic growth and high level of expatriates have contributed to the growth in the number of private institutions offering educational programmes. In addition to the higher education system institutions, local institutions operated at the emirate level and private institutions operating throughout the country have created a climate of competition for the best students. And with important strategic policy implications, in the aggregate these schools, over forty of them, enrol more students than does the UAE national higher education system (about 40,000 students).

Non-federal institutions and institutions in the free zones will provide additional access for Emiratis and this capacity should be taken into account when policies are determined for student access. Private-sector institutions may also offer UAE citizens the chance to pursue education in areas not available in the UAE system or at locations that are more convenient to their homes. This sector also permits students who did not pursue their studies immediately following graduation from secondary schools to have additional options for post-secondary educational experiences.

The UAE, through its ministry licensing system of the Commission for Academic Accreditation, has made a concerted effort to provide consumer protection through careful review of private institutional programmes that are on offer in the UAE. The Knowledge and Human Development Authority in Dubai is currently exploring quality assurance policies for institutions in its zones. A complex and growing system of higher education will require accurate and timely information to support it. A comprehensive database on higher education provides opportunities for better decision-making and an opportunity to demonstrate accountability of stated goals and objectives. As the UAE takes on additional challenges – providing students with better career counselling, making judgements about changes in curricula, or adopting new programmes – the need for data will increase. As its administrative responsibilities grow and the need for financial and other types of data expands, there will be a concomitant need to organise and manage the data so that it is useful to programme managers – so that it enjoys the confidence of top policymakers, and so that it illuminates the higher education system for all UAE citizens.

Also, it appears that higher education institutions could make better use of labour-market information in their planning for future programmes. In part, this may be due to the relatively modest amounts of labour-market information available. Efforts have been initiated to expand the range of information available; these have, however, not been brought to fruition because of lack of sufficient funding and changing priorities within the Ministry of Labour. However, data do exist which could be used, but, at present, collection, coordination and analysis of available data are dispersed and sporadic.[14]

Policy Implications

From the national perspective, the UAE has embarked on the path towards economic diversification which in the long run will render the UAE increasingly dependent upon an educated workforce. Energy-related income has and will provide the foundation, but sustainability of a non-petroleum economy is only possible with qualified employees. For Emiratis, a key factor is the increased capacity of the UAE's higher education system to provide access to quality programmes. Tertiary education capacity-building involves adequate facilities, instructional space such as laboratories and classrooms, IT and, most important, internationally qualified faculty. Budgeting for this requirement requires additional financial support from the federal government. All Emiratis do not have access to higher education because they might not have completed high school, they might lack English and mathematics skills or the federal universities lack space because of fiscal constraints.

Since federal allocations have remained relatively stable since 2000, and inflation and enrolment growth have exceeded spending effectiveness, increased funding is needed or enrolment caps need to be implemented. In fact, enrolment has been limited, with approximately 2,000 students being turned away in 2005/06. To achieve the major goal of providing access for Emiratis requires federal policies and action for increased funding. Delaying action limits student and national capacity to profit from and contribute to social and economic progress.

Higher education in the UAE now consists of federal campuses, private licensed institutions, free zone campuses, branch campuses, and non-federal emirate-level institutions and programmes – this results in a complex policy environment. The challenge is to benefit from the array of opportunities available to both Emiratis and expatriates, while aligning educational providers with the demands of the changing economy. The government of Dubai is addressing this through its Dubai Strategic Plan 2015 and the work of the Knowledge and Human Development Authority. Access is the paramount goal for the UAE and possibilities to achieve that are on the horizon. Comprising 20 per cent of the population, it is critical that Emiratis enrol in and graduate from college or university to have the opportunity of claiming their place in the economic structure and the future of the UAE. The education and development of its human resources are the key to the nation's prosperity for its citizens. The next generation of Emiratis deserves no less.

Notes

1. *Gulf News*, 14 May 2007, p. 38.
2. *The Economist*, 6 August 2005, p. 36.
3. *Jane's Defence Weekly*, February 2007, p. 38.
4. UAE Ministry of Higher Education and Scientific Research, *Higher Education and the Future of the UAE*, Abu Dhabi 2004.
5. UAE Ministry of Higher Education and Scientific Research, *Educating the Next Generation of Emiratis: a master plan for UAE higher education*, Abu Dhabi 2007.
6. Ibid.
7. Ibid.
8. UAE Ministry of Higher Education and Scientific Research, *Funding Students First: access to quality higher education programs in the United Arab Emirates*, Abu Dhabi 2004.
9. Ibid.
10. UAE Ministry of Higher Education and Scientific Research, *Higher Education and the Future of the UAE*, Abu Dhabi 2004.
11. Ibid.
12. UAE National Admissions and Placement Office, *Third Annual Survey of the No Shows*, Abu Dhabi 2004.
13. Abbas Abdelkarim and Hans Haan, 'Skills and Training in the UAE: the need for and the dimensions of institutional intervention', in *Policy Research Papers*, no. 5, Centre for Labour Market Research and Information, Dubai 2002, p. 17.
14. Abbas Abdelkarim and Hans Haan, 'Establishing a Labour Market Information System in the UAE: understanding the needs and identifying structures', in *Policy Research Papers*, no. 9, Centre for Labour Market Research and Information, Dubai 2002.

EIGHT

International Higher Education: ownership and opportunities – a case study of the British University in Dubai

David J. Lock

Introduction

The British University in Dubai (BUiD), was established by Law number 5 of 2003 of the Ruler of Dubai which was issued on 19 May 2003. The original idea for the university had emanated from the Dubai–UK Trade and Economic Committee (DUKTEC), which comprised nominees of the Dubai and UK governments. It was first thought that a British university would assist with the recruitment and retention of British expatriate workers, but a subsequent survey was inconclusive on this point, there being a good range of undergraduate provision in the emirate already and many undergraduates preferring to study away from home. Further discussions identified the opportunity for a research-based university to make a more substantial contribution to Dubai's development aspirations.

Formation

A group of founders in Dubai comprising the Al Maktum Foundation (the charitable trust of the ruling family), the Dubai Development and

Investment Authority (the 'development engine' of Shaikh Muhammad bin Rashid Al Maktum), the National Bank of Dubai, Rolls Royce International and the British Business Group of Dubai and the Northern Emirates came together. Significantly three of these bodies were UAE organisations and two were British. All pledged funding and together they petitioned the ruler for a decree.

The British Consul General in Dubai, the Director of the British Council in Dubai and the Vice Principal of the University of Edinburgh worked with this group to develop the concept and to organise a process which, in 2003, resulted in the universities of Edinburgh, Birmingham, Manchester and Cardiff agreeing to become BUiD's academic partners. Each of these universities had achieved a five or five-star ranking (denoting research of international significance) in the most recent UK Research Assessment Exercise in the discipline areas in which they were to relate to BUiD. This was considered to be necessary to enable BUiD to develop its research capability as quickly as possible. Each university was tasked with developing a single academic institute in BUiD connected to its area of strength. In 2005 City University of London was also selected to become an academic partner.

The British universities offered masters programmes in fields that were relevant to the economic development of Dubai and the wider Gulf region. They worked with BUiD's staff to contextualise these programmes for the Gulf region and to develop the necessary quality assurance and other structures necessary to achieve a licence from the Commission for Academic Accreditation of the UAE Ministry of Higher Education and Scientific Research. Such a licence would enable BUiD to operate as a UAE-based university and would provide it with accreditation eligibility for each of the academic programmes.

These universities also worked with the BUiD Registrar and Acting Chief Executive to appoint academic staff of equivalent calibre to their own who would then develop further and deliver these programmes and undertake research in Dubai. The staff appointed, all of whom were full-time employees of BUiD, were also given appropriate honorary academic recognition by the UK partner universities and were expected to work with their peers in the UK to develop their research. The UK universities also provided BUiD staff and students with learning resources and other benefits, including hosted visits that would enhance their experience.

Representatives of the UK universities regularly visited Dubai to assist with the establishment of BUiD and its promotion and to monitor the development and delivery of its programmes, so that they were satisfied that equivalent standards were being achieved and so that they could safeguard their academic reputations.

Additionally, the UK universities agreed to be the external examiners of their corresponding programmes in BUiD, so as to ensure that the standards achieved by the students in both countries were equivalent.

The specific BUiD Institutes and Masters Programmes offered in 2007 and their respective links with the UK Universities were:

- The University of Edinburgh – BUiD Institute of Informatics
    Information Technology*
    IT Management**
- The University of Birmingham – BUiD Institute of Education
    Education*
- The University of Manchester – BUiD Institute of Engineering
    Project Management*
    Human Resource Management
- Cardiff University – BUiD Institute of the Built Environment
    Sustainable Design of the Built Environment
- City University of London – BUiD Institute of Finance and Banking
    Finance and Banking

*   Programmes offered when the university opened in 2004.
**   With the University of Manchester supporting in the management area.

Governance

The formation of BUiD was overseen by a Provisional Council comprising representatives of the founders, the British Consul General, the Director of the British Council in Dubai, the Vice Principal of Edinburgh University and a representative of the Ruler's Court. It was chaired by Shaikh Ahmad bin Said Al Maktum, a member of the ruling family and the chairman of the Emirates Group and the Dubai Civil Aviation Authority. The majority of the council's members were British. The council functioned in accordance with a constitutional document that was based on that of a pre-1992, research-focused UK university.

After two years, in accordance with the constitutional document, the Provisional Council was reconstituted by the Ruler's Office as a University Council with a small majority of members now being UAE nationals. This was seen as a significant development indicating greater local 'ownership' of the development of BUiD while also retaining the essential partnership with UK interests. Academic governance was provided initially by an Academic Planning Group comprising representatives of the UK university partners and the BUiD Registrar. This was replaced in 2004 by a Senate comprising representatives of the British universities and heads of BUiD institutes with other senior BUiD staff. This likewise functioned in a similar way to the senate of a pre-1992 university.

Executive leadership was provided initially by a person experienced as a registrar and secretary in a UK university. He was supported by senior administrative colleagues in some cases recruited locally and in others appointed from international competition, or seconded from the UK partner universities. In February 2007 a UAE national was appointed as BUiD's first Vice Chancellor, on secondment from the United Arab Emirates University.

Advisory Structure

Initially, BUiD created an advisory group comprising representatives of Rolls Royce and human resource directors of a range of local organisations. This group provided advice on the initial range of programmes and market needs. As the BUiD institutes became more established there became a need for more specific advice for each institute and hence, in 2006, five advisory groups were formed to advise on the development of both the research and programme portfolios of their respective institutes. In addition they played a role in enabling the institutes to form closer relationships with relevant organisations in the sector. The central advisory group was dismantled in 2006.

Contributors

In addition to the founders, a range of other organisations contributed to BUiD in various ways. In 2007 they included:

- The Emirates Group
- Atkins
- Dubai Duty Free
- DUCAB (Dubai Cable Company (P) Ltd)
- The Emirates Foundation
- Hyder Consulting
- DUGAS (Dubai National Gas Co. Ltd)

In addition to these organisations, the government of Dubai provided funding and other resources and opportunities to BUiD.

Typically contributors would provide scholarships for students (with whom some developed relationships for mutual benefit which enriched the students' experience academically as well as financially), funded the appointment of staff or provided funding or opportunities for research and other benefits for staff or students. Representatives of half of the contributors also served on advisory groups, thereby making an input to the selection and development of new programmes.

In the case of one of the contributors, whereas the day-to-day engagement was with the senior staff of the Dubai office, the research that BUiD was undertaking attracted the attention of a British multinational's global head office, which resulted in it being promulgated in four other countries, thereby enriching the experience of the researchers and students involved very early in the life of the university. This resulted in opportunities for the leading students and staff in the form of travel, which contributed significantly to the international aspirations of the university. In addition to their financial support, the contributors played a valuable role in guiding the development of the university and keeping it in line with the economic development of Dubai and the region.

Relations with the Government of Dubai

BUiD received strong support in various forms from the government of Dubai. It became an integral part of Knowledge Village, an integrated learning community comprising fifteen different universities as part of a government strategy to create a higher-education cluster. Separately, it signed a memorandum of understanding with the Dubai Department of Economic Development with a view to guiding the preparation of a research strategy for the emirate. Later, following the establishment of the Dubai Knowledge and Human Development Authority (KHDA), the university received direct financial support from the KHDA and BUiD's Vice Chancellor became engaged in the development of a higher-education strategy for Dubai.

Stakeholders' Aspirations

Having introduced the various stakeholders it might be helpful to attempt to summarise the headline opportunities envisaged by each before proceeding to comment on the sustainability of the model.

Opportunities for Dubai and the UAE:
- Creation of intellectual capital to facilitate a knowledge-based society
- Training of skilled personnel
- Facilitating more Emiratis in achieving senior positions (and reducing the dependency on expatriates): training 'leaders of tomorrow'

- Education and HE system reforms
- Greater responsiveness to innovations and increased speed of development
- More effective and innovative organisations
- Creation of wealth for the UAE and the Gulf
- Improved quality of life
- British education in Dubai

Opportunities for the UK university partners:

- A gateway to the Gulf
- International intelligence
- Exchange opportunities (for staff and students) in both directions
- International research opportunities
- Collaborative opportunities
- Research
- Teaching
- Commercialisation of knowledge
- Dubai government agencies
- Dubai-based enterprises
- Revenue

Opportunities for founders and contributors:

- Exploitable research outputs
- Innovative scholars and graduates
- Public exposure through supporting BUiD
- Links with UK universities
- Links with other UK organisations
- Better networks
- Engagement in sustainable innovations and reforms

Opportunities for UK 'PLC':

- Flagship project status to focus on a region in the Middle East
- Trade links
- Student visits to boost awareness of the UK
- Joint research opportunities
- Gateway to UAE and the region
- Staff exchanges

Progress to Date

BUiD opened its doors to students in September 2004 when twenty-eight postgraduates registered on its three programmes after a very short period of marketing. Three years later, approximately 400 students have registered on BUiD's masters programmes, which now number seven, and which have been developed substantially. BUiD has over forty staff. Just over half of its students are UAE nationals and the others are nationals of twenty-eight different countries, resulting in a vibrant learning community. All of the reports submitted by independent UK-based external examiners have indicated that BUiD's students are achieving to a standard that is comparable to those of their counterparts in the UK partner universities. BUiD's academic staff have published over 100 papers in journals or conferences, and a handful of books.

Financially, BUiD started with foundation funds which were pledged by the founders. Other sources of funding have included student fees, revenue from scholarship providers, revenue from contributors in the form of the sponsorship of posts and income from specific research contracts from commercial bodies. Loan funding, funds from KHDA, assistance from a UK university partner through forgoing the fees due to it and contributions 'in kind' from the UK partners and other UK and Dubai bodies have enabled BUiD to operate to acceptable levels of quality at a time when the high costs of developing and staffing new programmes were being incurred ahead of any revenue from fees or the sponsorship of posts. The absence of funds presented challenges for research activity to develop as quickly as it might have done.

A comprehensive evaluation of the extent to which BUiD has managed to develop opportunities for its various stakeholders has yet to be undertaken. However, the growing number of students and the growing number of employers who are willing to fund their staff to participate in BUiD programmes and the continuation into subsequent phases of a major research project indicate confidence that value is being added. The donation of over 200 scholarships and the growing number of students and graduates achieving either promotion with their current employer or moving to more senior opportunities with other organisations would further suggest success.

BUiD's constant attention to sound British academic processes and achieving the standards of its UK university partners and the strict requirements of the UAE's Commission for Academic Accreditation have assured the well-qualified students who enter BUiD of a stimulating and vocationally relevant experience.

The recomposition of the governing body to create a majority of UAE nationals and the appointment of a UAE national to be chief executive of the university indicates a desire on the part of Dubai's government to exercise greater ownership and control over the university and its future development. The active involvement of the Vice Chancellor in the development of Dubai's higher-education strategy is evidence of BUiD's general engagement in the development of higher education in Dubai. The stream of international visitors, including representatives from higher education, regional government and industry, is evidence of the international reputation that BUiD has acquired to date.

BUiD has successfully bid to host two international conferences, one of which took place in November 2006 while the second was held in April 2008. This provides evidence that BUiD is capable of attracting staff from universities around the world and thereby assisting Dubai to achieve its aspiration of becoming the higher-education capital of the Gulf.

The involvement of two of BUiD's university partners in research and training opportunities in Dubai and plans for further engagement indicate BUiD's ability to deliver such opportunities. The decision of a UK multinational company to embark upon phases two and three of a research project that will extend the influence of research initiated in Dubai to other countries points to BUiD's international capability. The decision of a multinational Norwegian company, not previously connected with BUiD's creation or development, to partner with it in research which has significant application in the Middle East and which is expected to lead to that company establishing an operation in UAE, is evidence of BUiD having the potential to attract foreign direct investment into the UAE. The interest being expressed by a range of international professional bodies in collaborating with BUiD and, in some cases, seeing BUiD as a central point of contact for their UAE operations, points towards further benefits and opportunities for BUiD staff and students and for other professionals in the emirates, including easier access to opportunities for continuing professional development for professionals working in Dubai.

The continuing support of embassy officials by including relevant BUiD personnel in the reception of trade missions enhances BUiD's visibility internationally and its possible role in tipping the balance towards inward investment decisions being made in favour of Dubai. All BUiD's UK university partners have received payments in respect of the use of their intellectual property and their provision of quality assurance and other services. Two universities have received fees in respect of their engagement in research and training opportunities that BUiD has generated. All of this represents export earnings for the UK.

Conclusions

BUiD started out as a partnership between significant bodies in Dubai and the United Kingdom. Throughout its development, the relative strengths of its stakeholders and their representatives in the different countries have been employed to enable expertise, academics and other resources to be combined to deliver a high-quality experience for students and sponsoring organisations. Although the university is still very young, it would seem that the foundations have been laid to enable it to continue to develop and to achieve the aspirations held for it by its various stakeholders, not least the people and government of Dubai.

NINE

Quality Issues Affecting Higher Education in Bahrain

Khalil Y. al-Khalili

Bahrain is a relatively small country in both area (710 square kilometres) and population (708,573).[1] It also has the highest population density in the world, which is 1,066 person per square kilometre.[2] It has a well-developed communications and transportation network, which has allowed it to become a centre for banking and finance, and the headquarters for a number of multinational firms that do business in the Gulf region.

The social environment in Bahrain is highly attractive to foreign capital. Bahraini citizens are well educated; the illiteracy rate in the country is almost negligible: 1.4 per cent for males, 4 per cent for females and 2.7 per cent for both combined.[3] They are generally polite, friendly and respectful to others, especially those of different cultures. Foreigners find it highly encouraging to reside with their families in Bahrain, since they can find all kinds of facilities they like. In addition, Bahrainis value education very highly and are very enthusiastic when it comes to enrolling in training programmes and workshops. Each of the seven colleges of the University of Bahrain (the only national university) has a special department for offering such training programmes and workshops.

The government of Bahrain considers its people to be a most valuable asset. Human development is therefore of primary concern to the government. Thus 3.1 per cent of the gross national product is allocated for education. Offering the opportunity for high school graduates to proceed into higher education is of particular importance to the government of Bahrain. Higher education institutions were established for this purpose. There is one national university (the University of Bahrain); one regional university, which is the Arabian Gulf University (sponsored by the Gulf Cooperation Council); and two public higher education associations: the College of Health Sciences (affiliated to the Ministry of Health) and the Bahrain Training Institute (affiliated to the Ministry of Labour). Table 9.1 provides some details about each of these public institutions.[4]

Table 9.1. A List of Public Institutes in the Kingdom of Bahrain

No.	Institute Name	Starting Date	Number of Students 2007–2008*
1	University of Bahrain	1986	13,946
3	Arabian Gulf University	1979	900
3	College of Health Sciences	1976	1,200
4	Bahrain Training Institute	1992	3,500
	Total		19,546

* Source: F. H. Almulla Abdulla, *Higher Education in Bahrain*, paper presented to the Sixth Conference of the College of Education, University of Bahrain on 'Higher Education and Development Requirements: a futuristic perspective', 20–22 November 2007, Sakheer 2007.

Twelve private universities have been licensed and accredited. Together they serve about 12,000 students. Table 9.2 provides some details about each of these universities.[5] In addition, a further two private universities were recently licensed in October 2007.

Table 9.2. *List of Private Universities in the Kingdom of Bahrain*

No.	University Name	Starting Date	Number of Students 2006–2007
1	AMA International University of Bahrain	September 2002	2,299
2	The Gulf University	October 2002	191
3	Al-Ahlia University	February 2003	1,088
4	Arab Open University / Bahrain Branch	February 2003	2,100
5	University College of Bahrain	September 2002	529
6	Birla Institute of Technology International	September 2002	403
7	New York Institute of Technology (NYIT)	September 2003	1,182
8	The Kingdom University	September 2004	672
9	Applied Science University	September 2002	612
10	Delmon University for Science and Technology	July 2004	1,954
11	Bahrain Medical University Irish Surgery College	October 2004	219
12	The Royal University for Girls	September 2005	130
	Total		11,379

Higher Education: an investment in human resources

The wide and rapid expansion of private higher education institutions is considered an investment in human resources. These institutions offer an opportunity for high school graduates to select the field they wish to pursue their studies in. It can therefore be expected that these students will excel and graduate within the governmental institutions to prepare a qualified labour force that will participate in the development of the economy.

Another positive quality that distinguishes Bahraini society is that people in general have few negative attitudes towards what might be termed as 'shameful jobs'. Perhaps unlike some of the citizens of wealthier, oil-rich Gulf states, Bahraini citizens highly value and respect the jobs of their ancestors, such as diving for pearls. Certainly, today they do not hesitate to accept any kind of menial job such as farm worker, plumber or janitor. Thus, it is expected that graduates from private, as well as public, institutes will think freely about creating non-governmental jobs since it is impossible for any government to subsume huge numbers of graduates in the public sector.

It is anticipated that this investment in human resources in Bahrain will provide the country with valuable revenue in the future, raising the gross domestic product to a higher level. As an indicator of the progress of human development in Bahrain, Shaikh Khalifa bin Salman Al Khalifa, the prime minister of Bahrain for more than three decades, was granted the 2006 World Honour Prize for 'Distinguished Accomplishment in Human Development and Housing'. In addition, Bahrain has been awarded the top rank of the Arab countries in terms of human development for the past three years.

Quality Concerns about Higher Education in the Kingdom of Bahrain

Investment in higher education means that your product should be competitive with the products of others in both the private and public sectors. It is therefore essential that quality control is in place to ensure that your product is the best that it can be. The awareness of the importance of human resources as a valuable contribution to the income of Bahrain led the Economic Development Board to include education as one of the three pillars of reform in the country, the other two pillars being economic reform and the labour market. Quality was of central importance in the educational reform. Another concern about the quality of education at the university level stems from the rapid expansion of private universities and the wide range of programmes offered by these universities. Consequently, the Royal Decree number 3 for the year 2005 was issued for the establishment of a governmental institution named the Higher Education Council. The membership of this council consists of at least ten highly qualified professionals and scientific experts, amongst whom there must be representatives of both private and public higher education institutions. This council is in charge of licensing, accrediting and controlling higher educational institutions and programmes.

As part of the programme of education reform in Bahrain the Economic Development Board has taken the initiative of establishing a new institute named the Quality Assurance Authority (QAA). This is to be an independent governmental entity.[6] It was expected that this institution would be formally established early in 2008. The QAA will be responsible for controlling quality at all educational institutions, including universities. Four units will be associated with it: the Universities Inspections Unit, the Vocational Inspections Unit, the Schools Inspections Unit and the National Examinations Unit. The Australian Universities Quality Agency was selected as a partner with a local team for conducting quality audits. Experts from Australia were invited to provide workshops for Bahraini educators at different educational levels on self and external evaluation for quality.

How is the Quality of Higher Education Controlled in Bahrain?

The quality of higher education in Bahrain is controlled in a few different ways. These include, but are not limited to, the following:

1. Private universities have to fulfil a set of conditions and criteria to be licensed. Licensing is given at two different levels: general accreditation for practising their activities and specific accreditation for accepting students in specific programmes and degrees. These conditions and criteria are set by the Higher Education Council under the auspices of the Minister of Education.

2. In late 2007 the Higher Education Council formulated four official sets of by-laws that govern and control all higher education institutions. These are the Academic and Administrative By-laws,[7] the Building and Infrastructure By-laws,[8] the Financial By-laws[9] and the Regulations, Standards and Conditions of Licensure of Higher Education Institutes By-laws.[10]

3. The Higher Education Council has issued a decree that forces private universities to ready themselves for the fulfilment of the rules and regulations issued by the Council within a period of one academic year for the Academic and Administrative By-laws, and a period of three years for the requirements of the Building and Infrastructure By-laws.

4. The Economic Development Board arranged many workshops for senior officials from all universities in Bahrain to consider concepts of quality assurance in higher education and acquire techniques for effective self-evaluation of teaching and learning activities. An example of these was the one-day workshop on quality assurance and self-evaluation organised by the Universities Quality Review Project held in the summer of 2007.

5. All institutions were encouraged to get involved in programmes of quality assurance and enhancement supported by the government or international associations. The United Nations Development Programme supported a series of workshops arranged by the Quality Assurance Agency of the UK for the purpose of evaluating specific programmes at the University of Bahrain. This series goes back to early 2002 when two faculty members in the Department of Computer Science participated in a special workshop for preparing to assess the quality of the bachelors' degree programme in computer science. The assessment was performed by external audits, the results of which were generally good. In 2003 the Department

of Accountancy was involved in the same programme. The bachelors' degree programme in accountancy offered by this department was also evaluated for quality assurance, the results of which were also good in general. In 2006, the College of Education was also involved in the same programme. The postgraduate diploma in education was evaluated for quality assurance, the results of which were also good in general.

6. The University of Bahrain has also sent representatives to a series of activities arranged by the British Council on quality assurance and enhancement. These included a workshop held in Abu Dhabi in 2005, the Gulf states study tours in London during December 2006, and the 'methods and approaches to institutional audit' seminars held in Kuwait in January 2007.

7. Colleges are encouraged to seek accreditation for their programmes from international associations. Three out of the eight colleges of the University of Bahrain are working on this: the College of Education, which has prepared itself to gain accreditation from the National Council for Accreditation of Teacher Education, and the Colleges of Engineering and Information Technology, which are preparing themselves to gain accreditation from the Accreditation Board for Engineering and Technology.

8. The University of Bahrain and Al-Ahlia University (a private university) are now involved in a process of pilot testing the indicators and the process of evaluation for quality assurance by the Australian Universities Quality Agency with support from the Economic Development Board in Bahrain. The results of this evaluation will appear soon. This evaluation is considered as a trial stage in the overall evaluation of all higher education institutes in Bahrain. In the next academic year all private universities will be obliged to undergo the same process of evaluation for quality as those involved in trials.

Notes

1. Central Informatics Organisation (2007a). 'Bahrain in Numbers Statistics of 2004', retrieved 22 October 2007 from the web: http://www.cio.gov.bh/pdf/stat2004.pdf.
2. Encarta, 2007 'Bahrain Facts and Figures', retrieved 19 October 2007 from the web: http://Encarta.msn.com/fact_631504720/ Bahrain_facts_and_figures.html.
3. Central Informatics Organization (2007b). 'Bahrain in Numbers Statistics of 2001', Retrieved 22 October 2007 from the web: http://www.cio.gov.bh/default.asp?action=article&id=190.
4. F. H. Almulla Abdulla, *Higher Education in Bahrain*, paper presented to the Sixth Conference of the College of Education, University of Bahrain on 'Higher Education and Development Requirements: a futuristic perspective', 20–22 November 2007, Sakheer 2007.
5. A. Maawdeh, N. Hamoud, W. Al Khalifa and A. al-Tahmazi, *Academic Programmes Offered by Licensed and Unlicensed Private Higher Education Institutes*, Issa Town, Kingdom of Bahrain 2007 (in Arabic).
6. Economic Development Board, Universities Quality Review Project Overview Quality Assurance and Self-evaluation for Universities, Manama, Kingdom of Bahrain 2007 (in Arabic).
7. Higher Education Council, *Academic and Administrative By-laws*, Issa Town, Kingdom of Bahrain 2007a (in Arabic).
8. Higher Education Council, *Building By-laws*, Issa Town, Kingdom of Bahrain 2007b (in Arabic).
9. Higher Education Council, *Financial By-laws*, Issa Town, Kingdom of Bahrain 2007c (in Arabic).
10. Higher Education Council, *Regulations Standards and Conditions of Licensure of Higher Education Institutes By-laws*, Issa Town, Kingdom of Bahrain 2007d (in Arabic).

TEN

The Challenges of Vocational Training: BIBF, an institute of higher education

Mohammed Alkhozai

Higher education is a relative newcomer to the GCC states. The first university in the region was King Saud University, which was established in Riyadh, the Saudi Arabian capital city, in 1957, just over fifty years ago. Formal secular education on European models was only introduced in the first decades of the nineteenth century and the whole region was not exposed to modernisation before the First World War. The most common education at that time was Qur'anic education, conducted either at mosques, in what were known as 'circles', or in classes held at the homes of religious tutors, *mullas*, and was mainly aimed at youngsters. Credit for introducing modern education, at both primary and secondary levels, must go to the colonial administrations, with the exception of Saudi Arabia, which was not governed by a foreign power. A new era in the development of these societies was thereby ushered in.

All GCC countries were content with the first two stages of their educational system for some time until the 1960s when independence dawned in the region. New political, economical and social realities helped to advance higher education with the founding of Kuwait University, the second university in the Gulf, in 1966. It was established with the help of Egyptian expertise, the University of Cairo being a paradigm to be emulated. Most professions were taught at colleges that sought to train physicians, chemists, engineers, teachers and agronomists.

The need for vocational and professional training did, however, necessitate the introduction of special training institutes to meet the requirements of new industries, one of which was finance and banking. New developments in the economies of the GCC states occurred from the 1930s with the discovery of oil on the one hand and with the rise in oil prices in the 1970s with the oil boom on the other. The Gulf states experienced surpluses of funds and unprecedented wealth. Petro-dollars whetted the palates of banks and investors and hordes of international banks moved to the region to set up branches and offshore banking units to manage the surpluses in oil revenues.

These financial institutions required both local and expatriate manpower to run their businesses. There was a pressing need to recruit suitable applicants and a requirement to train these recruits to perform the required jobs to a sufficiently high standard. Vocational and professional institutes were therefore established to meet this need. The Bahrain Institute of Banking and Finance, better known by its acronym of BIBF, is one of these higher education institutes established to serve the new economy.

BIBF is one of the leading professional training institutes in Bahrain and the Gulf region. Founded in 1981 to provide essential training for the banking community in Bahrain, it has since evolved into an internationally recognised training and development organisation where over 100,000 students have attended courses since its inception. It is today the lead provider of training, education and professional development programmes to the financial industry in the Gulf. Although the banking and financial sectors still heavily utilise the institute, its education and training programmes are also offered to non-financial organisations in Bahrain and beyond. Over the years, its disciplines have altered to meet changing needs in training and education. Courses in management and leadership, Islamic banking and academic and executive education have been added to banking, finance and education.

The mission of BIBF has naturally had to change with changing times. Its primary mission is no longer simply to train the workforce in the financial industry; one of its major roles is to prepare and train the next generation of bankers, accountants and managers by providing adequate academic and professional education at both undergraduate and graduate levels. BIBF is a professional, world-class provider of performance improvement solutions to individuals, the financial services sector and other organisations, in their pursuit of excellence through life-long learning experience. Its declared intention is that it 'is the Institute of choice for the development of business professionals'.

Although the institute started by focusing on banking studies alone to cater for training needs of banking institutions in Bahrain in the early 1980s, it has evolved into a fully-fledged vocational and professional centre offering training and educational programmes through its six 'learning centres'. These centres provide training and education in the following disciplines:

- Banking
- Accounting and IT
- Insurance
- Leadership and management
- Islamic banking and finance
- Academic and executive education

Through these centres, students or trainees may attend short- or long-term programmes leading either to professional qualifications or to academic designations. As a result of its quality programmes, BIBF has been recognised as a provider of superior value, with uncompromisingly high levels of customer satisfaction and results oriented solutions. BIBF programmes have been tailored to suit a wide range of customers: devising targeted training programmes for both public and private bodies as well as educating individuals keen to acquire professional and academic qualifications or executive training. It also provides career planning assistance for newly appointed recruits. To ensure the continued quality of its programmes, BIBF employs highly qualified faculty members of diverse nationalities devoted to the advancement and enrichment of the human experience. The scale of the institute's activities is demonstrated by the approximate number of 13,000 participants who attended programmes of roughly 400,000 participant hours in 2006. Of these participants, 30 per cent came from outside Bahrain. Since its inception BIBF has provided instruction to participants from over fifty countries. It has also delivered programmes around the globe, including, for example, Saudi Arabia, Kuwait, Oman, UAE, Qatar, Malaysia, Indonesia and Sudan.

The institute's academic and professional programmes lead to qualifications that are internationally accredited by professional bodies or universities such as Chartered Financial Analyst (CFA), Chartered Certified Accountant (ACCA), Certified Public Accountant (CPA), Chartered Management Accountant (CMA), Certified Internal Auditor (CIA), Financial Risk Manager (FRM), Certified Accounting Technician (CAT), Associateship of Chartered Insurance Institute (ACII) and Chartered Property and Casualty Underwriter (CPCU). BIBF strives to partner with highly reputed institutions and organisations in the United States and the United Kingdom to offer world-class programmes to its clients. It also enjoys strategic relationships with internationally recognised professional organisations which deliver programmes jointly with BIBF. Among such organisations are, for example, the Federal Reserve Bank of New York, American Bankers Association, US Securities and Exchange Commission, NASDAQ, Darden Graduate School of Business (University of Virginia), DePaul University, Bentley College, University of Wales, University of Cambridge International Examinations, *ifs* School of Finance, Chartered Association of Certified Accountants and Chartered Insurance Institute.

Over the past twenty-six years, the institute has been serving the financial community in Bahrain and around the Gulf by addressing its training and development needs. Its corporate partners comprise a wide variety of organisations, ranging across the public and private sectors. They include Ahli United Bank of Bahrain, Banque Arabe pour le développement économique en Afrique (BADEA) in Sudan, Bosnia International Bank, Gulf Insurance Company in Kuwait, Insurance Commission in Jordan, Islamic Development Bank in Saudi Arabia, Oman International Bank, Saudi Aramco, Aluminium Bahrain and Emirates Insurance Company among many others.

Over nearly three decades, BIBF has developed from a tiny training institute with modest facilities into a fully fledged professional institute offering world-class learning and training in a friendly environment with state-of-the-art facilities. The number of students attending programmes has grown with the passage of time. In 1981 there were just 450 attendees in four rooms but eight years later the institute had more than doubled in size. By 2006 the number of classrooms had nearly doubled again and the number of students attending classes had risen more than six-fold.

BIBF is proud of its achievements. It is a provider of vocational, professional, academic and executive education, meeting the demands of industry and its members; it has a unique set-up and ownership and state-of-the-art facilities. It is a centre of excellence providing professional and vocational training and has alliances with international professional bodies and world reputed universities. It employs a highly qualified international faculty and has highly competitive admission requirements for degree and specialised programmes.

But BIBF is not complacent and is aware that some challenges remain if it is to survive in an increasingly competitive environment. It must maintain its position as a regional centre of excellence by maintaining the quality of its facilities and the programmes it offers by adopting the latest advances in technology and methodology. It must meet the demands of its clients at reasonable cost. It must attract high-calibre faculty and reward and retain its staff. It must expand to keep up with accelerating economic growth.

ELEVEN

The Contribution of the Kuwait Foundation for the Advancement of Sciences to Scientific Education and Training at the National, Regional and Global Level

Ali A. al-Shamlan

The measure of a nation's progress is generally indicated by the advancements made in science and technology, and the contributions made by research and education. Science and technology promote the optimal environment for living; education and training enhance multi-dimensional growth and advancement of society. The Kuwait Foundation for the Advancement of Sciences (KFAS) is a non-profit organisation established in 1976 by the Emir of Kuwait for the advancement of sciences, not only in Kuwait but also in the global context. The KFAS remains committed to scientific growth and development and provides support by means of financial contributions. Funds are received from Kuwaiti shareholding companies that contribute a share of their annual net profit for scientific development.

The KFAS' Role and Commitment to Scientific Development

The KFAS has made every possible effort during the last three decades to support the advancement of the sciences and progress in all domains of human life. Its activities are promoted by the following objectives, which have been identified by its board of directors:

- Nurturing national skills through research and training
- Attaining academic and scientific excellence and developing human resources through education and training
- Recognising, encouraging and enhancing intellectual development through grants and prizes
- Establishing and promoting scientific programmes at national and international levels
- Addressing national issues in order to trigger development
- Supporting intellectual and scientific endeavours of a high quality
- Preserving historical Arab and national heritage through relevant programmes
- Promoting cooperation with international bodies for enhanced growth and progress

The major role of the KFAS is embedded in its mission, which is focused on scientific development. It has emerged successfully by partnering scientific growth and development and providing support for:

- Scientific research
- Recognition of academic excellence
- Contribution to the national scientific infrastructure
- Promotion of social and cultural programmes

The KFAS's Support for Educational Initiatives

The KFAS encourages educational and research institutions in Kuwait to participate in activities that enhance their knowledge and keep them abreast of new developments. Its various activities are geared towards goals that include support for infrastructural development (such as laboratories, equipment, computers and so on) in addition to support for research projects, conferences, training courses, seminars, publication of books and other cultural activities. One of the KFAS's oldest programmes is the Awards Programme. This recognises scientists' meritorious contributions to research and the sciences, thus paying tribute to the country's elite.

Scientific Research Programmes

Realising the impact of scientific progress on modern development, the KFAS has made immense contributions to scientific programmes that are of national significance. These have included:

- A research funding programme
- A water resources programme
- An environment and pollution programme
- A petroleum and energy programme

The total KFAS research funds awarded to scientific research projects in the past three decades amount to about $75 million dollars for an aggregate of 632 research projects in basic and applied sciences as well as in other areas of national strategic relevance.

Table 11.1. Research Funding in Three Decades

Areas	Research Projects	(US $)
Biological Sciences	78	11,470,808
Engineering Sciences & Technology	168	19,696,337
Medical Sciences	102	10,585,753
Natural Sciences	87	9,354,150
Social Sciences & Humanities	180	11,731,724
Assigned Projects	17	11,757,231
TOTAL	632	74,596,003

In addition, the KFAS has also recognised scientific excellence through special awards and prizes for meritorious scientific work. Major annual Awards for Excellence in Research and Sciences are as follows: the Kuwait Prize ($1,000,000), the Scientific Production Prize ($200,000), the Arabic Book Fair Prize ($110,000), the Islamic Organisation for Medical Sciences Prize ($40,000), the Distinguished Research Prize ($33,000) and the Agricultural Prize ($33,000).

Scientific Training, Seminars and Conferences

The KFAS has played a significant role in training Arab scientists at the Abdul Salam International Centre for Theoretical Physics (ICTP) in Italy. The KFAS, in association with the Arab School for Science and Technology, has conducted several workshops in Syria, Morocco, Bahrain, Qatar, Egypt, Lebanon and Kuwait with the purpose of bringing together Arab scientists on a common platform for mutual exchange of scientific ideas. At the local level, the KFAS set the ground for the scientific training of nationals by contributing to the purchase of the Observatory ($830,000) at the Science Club and the Electron Microscopy Unit at Kuwait University ($1,400,000).

The KFAS initiated training in international business and management under the Kuwait Programme at Harvard University for Gulf executives which is aimed at promoting understanding of the impact of global strategic, technological, economic and social trends on the Gulf nations.

Priority was also given to organising several national and international conferences and symposiums which provide unique opportunities for concerned personnel to train themselves and discuss as well as confront issues of vital significance to the region and the world.

Support for Scientific Infrastructure

The KFAS has played a significant role in contributing to the development of the national scientific infrastructure.

Table 11.2. Major Contributions to National Scientific Infrastructure

	US $
The Scientific Centre	107,581,472
Diabetes Centre	58,527,655
Centre of Excellence, Kuwait University	1,000,000
Facilities for Computer Education (Ministry of Education)	17,000,000
Electronic Microscope at Kuwait University Lab	1,445,000
Science Club (observatory, optical library)	1,207,000
Facilities for Special Needs Children (Ministry of Education)	1,522,741
Science Museum	261,800
Total	188,545,668

Support for Institutional Research

The tremendous support that has been extended to national institutions for the advancement of academic as well as research activities is as follows:

Table 11.3. KFAS Contributions to Institutional Research

	US $	Number of projects
Kuwait Institute for Scientific Research	29,645,735	215
Kuwait University	13,838,685	208
Public Authority for Applied Education & Training	2,376,921	47
Ministry of Health	1,544,912	24
Others	27,189,149	138

Technical Innovation and Skills

The KFAS's support for the Science Olympiads set the direction for young scientists to utilise and excel in technical skills and participate in international competitions. Since 1978 many science students from Kuwait, between sixteen and twenty-four years of age, have benefited from the London International Youth Science Forum as participants and winners of national and international science competitions and science fairs. At the national level, the KFAS has contributed $17 million for supporting a children's computer education programme and for the enhancement of hardware, software and the curriculum, thus benefiting 60,000 kindergarten and 100,000 intermediate students and 600 teachers from 170 public schools.

The recent international recognition received for the accomplishments of the Kuwait Inventors' Bureau demonstrates the world-class expertise of our young inventors that was tapped and brought into the limelight through support and training.

Support for information dissemination through publications (50,000 books), media, libraries and exhibitions has also played a significant role in education and training.

The KFAS has joined forces with the UNESCO office in Egypt and the Arabian Gulf University in Bahrain in order to organise management training programmes in science and technology under the STEMARN (Science and Technology Management Arab Regional Network) programme.

Establishment of Centres of Excellence

The contribution made towards the establishment of the Centre of Excellence at Kuwait University was undertaken primarily to promote training in the administrative sciences. The KFAS set up the Scientific Centre which is dedicated to lifelong training with state-of-the-art facilities for all ages at the modern day Aquarium, Discovery Place, IMAX Theatre and the Dhow Harbour.

The establishment of the world-class Dasman Centre for Research and Treatment of Diabetes constitutes a major milestone in scientific development, which addresses diagnostic and therapeutic purposes and promotes clinical and biomedical research and education.

Overseas Collaboration for Scientific Development

The KFAS supports scientific initiatives and programmes directed towards development in the areas of science and technology at both regional and international levels. The Kuwait Programme at Harvard University initiated in 2001 is a strategic partnership between the KFAS and the John F. Kennedy School of Government at Harvard University, which serves the leaders and decision-makers of various Kuwaiti institutions from the private and public sectors through unique opportunities for cooperation on advanced research, teaching, training and outreach on critical issues.

The KFAS has signed an agreement with the Massachusetts Institute of Technology to establish the Centre for Natural Resources and Environment which is tasked to seek unique opportunities for understanding and addressing key issues related to the management of petroleum and water resources and the protection of the natural environment.

The Kuwait Programme on Development, Governance and Globalisation in the Gulf States in cooperation with the London School of Economics promotes a prestigious multi-disciplinary global programme and includes high-level scholarly research on priority topics, academic exchanges, seminars and conferences.

The Kuwait Programme at Le Fondation Nationale des Sciences Politiques (Sciences-Po) is a multi-purpose programme aimed at enhancing research and expertise capacity on global matters, comprising a professorship, a research programme, fellowships, executive training programmes and enhancement of the Menton Programme ('Leaders for Tomorrow').

The KFAS's contribution of $600,000 towards the Third World Academy of Sciences represents immense support for the advancement of science in the developing world.

The KFAS also supports the Abdul Salaam International Centre for

Theoretical Physics which aims to provide scientists in the Arab region with opportunities to conduct research and to study new developments in physics and mathematics as well as applied and related fields of science.

The Kuwait Mathematics Programme at the University of Cambridge, sponsored by the KFAS, supports advanced studies and research in number theory as well as research posts, scholarships and lectures by eminent international mathematicians, with the purpose of establishing a unique link between Cambridge mathematicians and Arab mathematicians, highlighting and spreading their work and thus expanding research in the area.

The KFAS set up an endowment with a total of £2,500,000 at the Oxford Centre for Islamic Studies, which creates a new dimension in traditional Islamic studies by providing opportunities for Muslim scholars to participate in international programmes, seminars and competitions, thus benefiting from a prestigious world academy. At the same centre, the KFAS also established the Kuwait Library with an initial contribution of £6,000,000 and then a further £216,200 for the operational phase.

In 2005 the Arabian Gulf University in Bahrain was endowed with $2,500,000 for the Kuwait Academic Chair at the Department of Clinical Microbiology and Immunology in honour of the late Emir.

The KFAS also contributed to the James Baker Institute for Public Policy and the Chair for Arab Studies at Rice University.

The KFAS's endowment supports a chair in the Elliot School of International Affairs at George Washington University for studies on Gulf and Arabian Peninsula Affairs.

Table 11.4. Summary of Contributions to
Ongoing International Programmes

Institutes	KFAS Contributions (US$)
Harvard University	8,200,000
Massachusetts Institute of Technology	11,500,000
London School of Economics	11,662,910

Institutes	KFAS Contributions (US$)
Le Fondation Nationale des Sciences Politiques	6,659,836
Third World Academy of Sciences	600,000
The Abdul Salaam International Centre for Theoretical Physics	819,672
Cambridge University	2,605,124
Oxford Centre for Islamic Studies	27,082,377
Arab School of Science & Technology	950,000
Arabian Gulf University	2,500,000
Rice University	700,000
George Washington University	3,500,000
TOTAL	76,779,919

Conclusion

The KFAS will steer and act as a catalyst for scientific progress in order to maintain a sustainable future not only for the nation but for the region and the world at large.

Its vision for the future is focused on its priorities, which will hopefully trigger greater development in the entire Gulf region. The KFAS will promote the maximum utilisation of natural resources, enhance human resources, and promote better scientific facilities for good living. It will work in partnership with international scientific bodies to realise our dreams, we will visualise a better future beyond the promising horizons of science and knowledge and we shall strive to promote global changes with greater thrusts and challenges, as we move rapidly into the twenty-first century.

TWELVE

The Potential Contribution of GCC Universities to International Development

Digby Swift

A university is a community of scholars and teachers. Their task is to push forward the boundaries of knowledge, ideas and creativity, and to share their knowledge, experience, skills and creativity with others. They have a duty to their founding community, whether national, secular or religious. But great universities have also prized their freedom to pursue global scholarship, in partnership with others, for the benefit of the global community. Wealthier universities have a privileged opportunity and duty to support those in poorer countries. This might be through partnership with fellow universities, through contracts with governments and development agencies, or more directly though the orientation of their research and through external students. There are already a number of examples of this, past and present, and there are undoubtedly ways in which this can be readily taken forward by the universities of the GCC.

International Development: a university goal
from the earliest times

The Alexandria Library was founded *circa* 283 BC.[1] It housed over half a million documents on 'global development' in terms of international politics and culture. Given that it employed over 100 scholars, it can also be considered one of the world's first universities. Its primary purpose was to apply Aristotle's techniques and Greek thought to the learning of Greece, Egypt, Macedonia, Babylonia and beyond, in order to provide a better understanding of Greece's citizens and trade partners.[2] The rise and fall of the Alexandria Library provides a lesson for modern universities. Whilst its growth came from a commitment to global issues, its destruction may have been a result of inward-looking national politics and sectarianism. Plutarch blamed Julius Caesar for burning it down. The atheist Gibbons blamed the first Christians. Bishop Gregory blamed the Muslim Caliph Omar.

A modern university can raise its eyes to the world and contribute scholarship, training and resources to questions of global development, inequality and deprivation. Or it can turn inwards and lose itself in narrow – albeit immediate and demanding – national, logistical and proprietary issues. New universities have much to cope with: rapid growth, staffing, new courses and resources, balancing national labour market needs and student aspirations and satisfying the demands of the university's sponsors. At the same time, however, they also have a wider duty to the international community: reducing global deprivation and strengthening global understanding and partnership.

GCC Universities Have Much to Offer

Many of the universities in the GCC states are well resourced and have modern facilities. Far more so than the Alexandria Library, they operate in a region of rapid change, of booming economies, of major political questions and in a changing civil society. They are also juxtaposed between East and West, they are homes to aspects of Arab, European and Asian heritage, and, for some, they have become a focal point for religious inspiration. Many are already directly linked to major international universities and all have good access to global academia. Many already have a global developmental vision.

There Are Many Ways for Universities to Support International Development

Universities can help to tackle global poverty and other disadvantages by providing access for poorer countries and communities to training courses, notably those that will qualify new teachers, doctors and engineers. Research at universities in the GCC could be at the forefront of economic, political and scientific analysis of global problems and trends, assessing options and identifying, evaluating and disseminating good practice. Moreover, universities can be an effective challenge to governments and the international community by providing factual evidence to lobby for greater commitment to the world's poorer citizens, and by monitoring their performance in meeting these commitments.

Universities can help international development through a commitment to train and inspire students from a wide background. They can adopt a global intake, and can avoid all entry discrimination other than on academic grounds. They can shun 'ivory towers', entering the 'real world' of the students and inspiring students to question and seek constructive solutions to real-life problems.

Courses can emphasise the relevance of their subject matter to national global development. Teaching can be made directly relevant to the students, and their communities, with an emphasis on the practical and applied. Special courses, workshops and materials can be initiated on development-related issues. Staff interests in global development can be fostered, especially in terms of research and facilitating external consultancy work for development agencies. Libraries can encourage the gathering and dissemination of information on international development and campaigns for action by the wider community.

The university community as a whole can include direct outreach activities to the local and global community. These can range from voluntary support to locally disadvantaged groups, through support to international development agencies and organisations, to direct action in poorer countries that need support for higher education.

An Early Example of a Transnational, Developmental Vision

Al-Azhar, in Egypt, is one of the oldest universities in the world still operating. It was founded in 975 AD. It is open to all Muslims, and all students enjoy the same rights as native Egyptian students. Its mission is to provide Egypt and the Islamic world with scholars and experts who are well equipped to discuss and apply Islamic culture and ethics, and are well prepared to serve their societies, and can then play their role in building up their countries on a faith and scientific basis.[3] The university seeks to prepare a stock of leading and highly qualified academicians and scientists for the coming generation in all branches of knowledge and experience required for both the spiritual and material sides of life. Scholarship in various walks of life is intended to offer the best experience possible in the interest of Egypt and all Muslims in the entire Muslim world. Academic relations are encouraged with universities and research foundations all over the world.

Transcending Creedal and Gender Restrictions – UCL[4] and Ahlia[5]

Religions have throughout history been major supporters of scholarship and learning. But this has often restricted their impact, notably in terms of sectarian and gender limitations. For example, 180 years ago, English university education was only available to members of the Church of England, and primarily male members. University College London was founded to provide a progressive alternative. It was the first university in England to admit students of any race, class or religion, and the first to welcome women on equal terms with men. It included overseas students from the start, and established a teaching programme in which religious beliefs would not constrain the dissemination of knowledge and exploration of ideas. Academic disciplines were introduced as required by the emerging industrial and commercial society. These included the subjects of law, architecture and medicine.

Ahlia University in Bahrain is a university in the GCC which has a similar mandate to UCL. Admission is based only on academic achievement regardless of race, colour, gender, religion, nationality and disabilities.

Increasing the Relevance of Science and Technology to Equitable Development – Kenyatta University[6]

Universities are often seen as bastions of privilege and elitism – ivory towers, high above the concerns of the poor. Yet many universities have gone out of their way to reach the poor, and to increase the relevance of their courses to equitable development.

Kenyatta University is an example of a university that has laid a stress on equitable development. Its vision is 'to provide quality education and training, promote scholarship, service, innovation and creativity and inculcate moral values for sustainable individual and societal development'. Kenyatta University is Kenya's second university and was born out of the education department of the original Nairobi University. I was head of physics at Kenyatta in the early 1980s, when the university was developing new courses and a new programme of research. I remember vividly one initiative to reach teachers of *madaaris* (religious schools) and other schools in the poorest, most drought-stricken areas of Kenya. Several staff members were concerned at the low relevance for the people of Kenya of the science courses at school level, and much of the scientific research in both Nairobi and Kenyatta universities. As 'appropriate technology' was then the much-publicised term for reaching the poor through science and technology, we established the Appropriate Technology Centre for Education and Research. This was initially a research unit and base for workshops and general outreach covering both science education and science and technology research. The science education theme fed into the university and schools courses a number of examples of rural development and technology used by the informal sector. These examples were used to introduce and apply scientific concepts.[7] The scientific research had an applied science emphasis, linking with Nairobi University engineering departments. The emphasis was partly on low-cost construction and on energy technology, notably solar energy, wind energy, biogas and stoves. A number of technical spin-offs fed into the work of a number of development agencies. This initiative in due course fed into the new Department of Engineering and Technology. This had its own students and undertook research relevant to low-income groups. It still has active links with local industries and organisations. Every year, its students undergo field attachments in local industries and government bodies. Informal sector commercial enterprises are encouraged to take part in joint ventures and collaborations.

Moving Universities into New Areas of International Concern – the Bradford University Department of Peace Studies

Like several other British universities, Bradford University has a long tradition of contributing to international development. One example is the Bradford University Centre for International Development.[8] This is a leading centre for development studies with students from over 120 countries taking degrees in, for example, economics, business economics and international economics, development studies, international relations, sociology, social policy, psychology and marketing. The centre also has a research programme focusing on resources, livelihoods and development policies, plus seminars and consultancies.

One unique aspect of the centre is its Department of Peace Studies. This is the largest department for the study of peace and conflict in the world. It began with support from the Religious Society of Friends (the Quakers), a body committed to peace and non-violent resolution of conflict.[9] It set up and funded the department's first chair in 1973.

As a new field of initiative for a university, the department had a number of difficult issues to tackle. The definition and development of a broad understanding of peace was only one of these. The concept had to be organised into a practical programme of teaching and research, with a coherent assessment system linked to the teaching and an internal organisation, including staff-student relations. The department is now as large as many mainstream social science departments with twenty-two staff, eighty undergraduates, postgraduate studies and research, and a full publishing programme. Moreover, there are five research centres within the department concerned with peace and conflict studies, disarmament research, conflict resolution, international cooperation and security and participation studies. The department's research outcomes provide both support for government and civil society initiatives, and a means of evidence-based lobbying for peace.

Community Service Programme at the American University in Cairo[10]

The American University in Cairo (AUC) was founded in 1919 as an English-medium university. It is an independent, non-profit, apolitical, non-sectarian and equal-opportunity institution. Its high input of consultancy and research facilities to international development activities and its strong publishing house have served the international community well. From the outset, there was a commitment to citizenship and service, and increasingly a shared commitment to service and a common vision to improve Egypt, the region and the world, and to compel faculty and students on the campus to offer their time and energy to serve others.

Established in 2006 in honour of a former AUC president, the John D. Gerhart Center for Philanthropy and Civic Engagement was designed to consolidate university activities aimed at encouraging engaged citizenship and service, and to promote philanthropy in the Arab world. Combining learning, research, service and advocacy, the Center works to expand the boundaries of philanthropy, moving it beyond mere charity towards social justice and development. The Center is ensuring that AUC's contributions to society will go well beyond its campus borders.

Through its service-learning initiative, AUC blends service activities with academic courses, making community service an integral part of the students' learning experience. AUC's growing number of service-learning courses enables faculty members to integrate community service into their curriculum, demonstrating that the lessons learned in the classroom add real value to the community. Through these courses, students help educate local high school students about public and personal health issues, and work to provide counselling to families whose children are being treated at the National Cancer Institute in Cairo.

From raising money to building a library in an underprivileged village to hosting an on-campus party for orphans, AUC students are actively engaged in establishing and running community service clubs that work with the elderly, cancer patients, orphans and the poor. The university's Community Service Programme connects service-based student clubs with NGOs and other agencies to provide a far-reaching and long-term range of services and activities that targets the needy.

Partnering Universities in Low-income Countries: UCL's relationship with Makerere University, Uganda[11]

Several of the GCC's universities are now well established. Many of the newer GCC universities are offshoots or external campuses of universities in the US, Europe or Australia. Hopefully they will soon be able to support other universities and research in low-income countries.

University College London has been working with and supporting Makerere University since its foundation in the 1930s, through its transition from Uganda Technical College to a higher education institute in 1937, as an affiliated college of UCL in 1949, as the University of East Africa in 1963 and since its transition to a fully independent university in 1970. Up until 1970, Makerere was offering UCL degrees, and throughout the 1970s several British teachers were being trained at Makerere University, teaching for a short time in Uganda before returning to teach in the UK on the same basis as if they had taken their PGCE course at UCL. Arthur Tattersall was the

Deputy Academic Registrar of UCL from 1950 to 1955 and Secretary of UCL from 1964 to 1978. From 1955 to 1961 he served as Secretary of Makerere at the time that UCL was supervising Makerere.[12]

Now that Makerere University is well established with many global links, it still partners UCL in a number of development research projects. One example is the Uganda Women's Health Initiative[13] between Makerere University, Mulago Hospital and the Institute for Women's Health at UCL. Another example is related to global climate change, with a project entitled 'Climate Change and the Aquatic Ecosystems of the Ruwenzori Mountains'.[14]

Learning Lessons from the Alexandria Library

Regardless of exactly who or what destroyed the Alexandria Library, narrow political or sectarian agendas are likely to have played a role. Are contemporary universities also fostering such divisive, competitive agendas?

Or are contemporary, established universities centres for global enlightenment, collaboration and development? Is there scope for greater emphasis on global development issues, addressing global inequity and suffering? Can they be, like the Alexandria Library, a means of learning from all and applying the best that each nation, community or religion can contribute to a better, fairer future?

Notes

1. Preston Chester, 'The Burning of Alexandria Library', ehistory archives, http://ehistory/world/articles/ArticleView.cfm?AID=9.
2. Ellen N. Brundige, 'The Library of Alexandria', http://www.perseus.tufts.edu/GreekScience/Students/Ellen/Museum.html.
3. 'Al-Azhar University, Cairo. The world's oldest university and Sunni Islam's forefront seat of learning', http://www.islamfortoday.com/alazhar.htm.
4. University College London website: http://www.ucl.ac.uk/about-ucl.
5. Ahlia University website: http://ahliauniversity.edu.bh/home.htm.
6. Kenyatta University website: http://www.ku.ac.ke/.
7. Digby Swift, *Physics for Rural Development*, Oxford 1983.
8. Bradford University website: www.bradford.ac.uk/acad/bcid.
9. James O'Connell and Simon Whitby, 'Constructing and Operating a

Department of Peace Studies at the University of Bradford: a reflection on experience between 1973 and 1995', http://www.brad.ac.uk/acad/peace/about/history.pdf.

10. American University in Cairo website: http://www.aucegypt.edu/aboutauc/Pages/default.aspx.

11. Makerere University website: http://mak.ac.ug/makerere/.

12. Negley Harte, 'Arthur Tattersall: deft Secretary of University College London', *The Independent*, 30 July 2005.

13. http://www.instituteforwomenshealth.ucl.ac.uk/InternationalProjects/inaugural_conference.

14 http://www.geog.ucl.ac.uk/~rtaylor/rwenzori.htm.

Notes on Contributors

Mohammed Alkhozai is Head of the Academic and Executive Learning Centre at the Bahrain Institute of Banking and Finance and is responsible for managing degree programmes, executive development and education programmes at the Bahrain Institute of Banking and Finance (BIBF). Previously, he held the position of Director of Culture and Arts and Director of Publications at the Ministry of Information in Bahrain. He has also lectured in English at the Teacher Training College in Bahrain. Mohammed Alkhozai graduated with a BA in English Literature from the University of Cairo and received his master's degree from the School of English at the University of Leeds. He obtained his doctorate from the School of Oriental and African Studies at the University of London, specialising in comparative literature and Arabic drama. Dr Alkhozai is a member of a number of professional and learned societies including the British Society for Middle Eastern Studies, Middle East Studies Association of North America, Bahrain Management Society, Bahrain Society for Training and Development and the Bahrain Historical and Archaeological Society. He is a member of the Board of Trustees of the University of Bahrain and is a past member of the National Council for Culture, Arts and Literature, and a past President of both the Oruba Club and the Bahrain Chess Federation. He has published and translated a number of books and has also written on dramatic and literary criticism.

Jane Bristol-Rhys is an anthropologist who teaches Emirati social history and cultural heritage at Zayed University in Abu Dhabi where she is an assistant professor in the Department of Humanities and Social Sciences. Her research examines Emirati perspectives on the changes that have transformed their society and efforts to re-define and maintain Emirati identity. Her book, *The Width of my Burqah: change, loss and tradition*, is to be published soon by Hurst and Co.

Christopher Davidson is a fellow of the Institute for Middle Eastern and Islamic Studies at Durham University, and a former assistant professor of political science at Zayed University in Abu Dhabi and Dubai. A policy expert on the Gulf states, he is the author of *Dubai: the vulnerability of success* (Columbia University Press) and *The United Arab Emirates: a study in survival* (Lynne Rienner Press). He has published articles in several academic journals including *Middle East Policy*, *Asian Affairs* and *Middle Eastern Studies*, and has worked extensively with leading consultancy companies including PA, Oxford Analytica and the Oxford Business Group.

Warren H. Fox is Executive Director of Higher Education for the Knowledge and Human Development Authority of the Government of Dubai. He also serves on the School Board for the American Community School. Previously Dr Fox served as Scholar in Residence, University of California at Berkeley, with the Center for Studies in Higher Education, and has served as Executive Director of California's planning and coordinating agency for higher education and acted as convener of the California Education Roundtable, composed of California's university system leaders. As Vice Chancellor for Academic Affairs for the University and Community College System of Nevada, he led educational policy and planning for the universities and community colleges. Dr Fox has travelled extensively and has served as a delegate of the Carnegie Foundation for the Advancement of Teaching to the People's Republic of China, as well as acting as a consultant to the Centre for Higher Education Policy Studies in the Netherlands. Dr Fox received his BA in Political Science from the University of California at Berkeley, and his PhD from the

University of Southern California School of Policy Planning and Development.

Moudi al-Humoud has been President of the Arab Open University (AOU) since September 2004. She received a BSc in Business Administration (High Honours) from Kuwait University in 1972, an MBA degree in Business Administration Management from North Texas State University in 1976 and a PhD in Business Administration from City of London University in 1979. Dr al-Humoud has had a varied academic career at Kuwait University. She has had ties with the International Institute of Administrative Sciences (IIAS) in Brussels as Chairman of its Public Enterprise Research Committee and is a registered qualified expert at the Gulf Cooperation Council's GCC Commercial Arbitration Centre. She is a member of the Editorial Board of the *Journal of Administrative Sciences, Kuwait University*, and is Chief Editor of the *Journal of Sciences of Kuwait University*. Dr al-Humoud has published two textbooks and many different papers in the field of leadership and organisations. She is a member of the Higher Council of Planning and Development in the State of Kuwait.

Khalil Y. al-Khalili is Dean of the College of Education at the University of Bahrain and Editor in Chief of *JEPS*, the *Journal of Educational & Psychological Sciences* at the university's College of Education. He has held many academic posts, has led a team assigned by the World Bank for preparation of science curricula for teaching programmes in the Republic of Yemen and has acted as Consultant to the Rashid Bin Humaid Award for Science and Culture. Professor al-Khalili has published more than forty-five articles in international and national, refereed scientific journals and has co-authored fifteen books. He holds a PhD in Science Education and an MSc in Science Teaching from the University of Illinois and a BSc in Physics from the University of Jordan.

David J. Lock was appointed as Director of International and UK Projects at the Leadership Foundation for Higher Education in London in October 2007. Prior to then he was the founding Registrar and Acting Chief Executive of the new British University in Dubai, a post he held for four years where his brief was to structure and build the university from scratch, lead the university and manage relationships with the UK university partners and UAE Government and other stakeholders, achieve UAE programme accreditation, raise funds, develop new programmes and activities while ensuring UK standards were met, increase the student population, and to establish and enhance the reputation of the university in the UAE and internationally. Before going to Dubai David Lock had served as Secretary to the University of Huddersfield, and Registrar and Secretary to the University of Hull in the UK, for a total of fourteen years. His first profession is that of a teacher. He is also a Fellow of the Institute of Chartered Secretaries and Administrators and an adviser to the Institute. He is a Freeman of the City of London and Liveryman of the Worshipful Company of Chartered Secretaries and Administrators. He has also undertaken a range of consultancy assignments including national higher education governance projects, including the training of members of governing bodies at national level and further-education governance assignments.

Mari Luomi works for the International Politics of Resources and the Environment programme in the Finnish Institute of International Affairs. She is currently writing a doctoral thesis on the energy security and climate change attitudes of small Gulf states at the Institute for Middle Eastern and Islamic Studies at the University of Durham. Luomi obtained her bachelor's and master's degrees in International Relations from the University of Helsinki, Finland. She has written and contributed to different publications of the Finnish Institute of International Affairs and the Finnish Ministry of Defence on International Relations in the Middle East and Shiʻi-Sunni relations at the regional level.

Peter Mackenzie Smith is a consultant on international education and training and a Director of Getenergy Ltd. Earlier in his career he worked with the British Council including two periods at the British Council's office in Cairo, from 1972 to 1977 and 1983 to 1987. Subsequently he had global responsibility for the council's education and training development projects and for the promotion of UK education internationally. From 1997 to 2003 he was Director of Education at GEC plc and Marconi. He has recently directed a series of five strategic forums on education and the countries of the Middle East, in London, Abu Dhabi and Cairo.

André Elias Mazawi is an Associate Professor in the Department of Educational Studies at the University of British Columbia where his work is focused upon critical sociology of education. He is interested in the intersection of geopolitics and globalisation, exploring their impact upon schooling, educational policies and school restructuring reforms. His published research focuses more particularly upon the debates and controversies surrounding the notion of a 'knowledge society' and 'education for work' in Arab societies, their sources, institutional origins and discursive reproduction across space. He is also exploring how cultural, ideological and political frameworks inform and shape discourses on educational policies and restructuring reforms across the Arab region. Dr Mazawi has published two books: *Pathologizing Practices: the impact of deficit thinking on education* with C. Shields and R. Bishop, and *Between State and Church: life-history of a French-Catholic school in Jaffa* with O. Ichilov, and has contributed articles to many books and journals devoted to education in the Arab world.

Ali A. al-Shamlan is one of the Founding Fellows of the Islamic Academy of Sciences (1986) and has been Director General of the prestigious Kuwait Foundation for the Advancement of Sciences (KFAS) since 1985. Throughout his career he has acted as a scientific leader, steering his nation towards scientific excellence and advancement. A specialist in the subject of geology, Professor al-Shamlan earned his doctorate degree in 1973 from the University of Kuwait, his MSc degree from the University of Texas at El Paso (1971) and B.Sc degree from the University of Puget Sound, USA (1967). In 2001 he was awarded an honorary doctorate from the University of Massachusetts, Amherst. Essentially a scientist and educationist by profession, he has held senior posts in scientific, academic and governmental institutions. He was Minister of Higher Education from 1988 to 1992, Dean (1982–4) and Assistant Dean (1978–82) of the Faculty of Sciences, Kuwait University and Chairman of its Geology Department (1975–8). He is the author of several scientific papers, including a book on geology. He is also a member of several world-renowned organisations.

Gregory Starrett is Professor of Anthropology at the University of North Carolina at Charlotte where he teaches classes on religion, the Middle East and the history of anthropology. A graduate of Stanford University, he studies Islam, media and politics in Egypt, among African American Muslims in the United States and in the larger Muslim world. He is the author of *Putting Islam to Work: education, politics and religious transformation in Egypt* (University of California Press, 1998), which examines the use of religious education programmes in state schools and their connection to state politics and popular Islamic movements. He has recently edited a new book, along with Eleanor Doumato of Brown University, entitled *Teaching Islam: textbooks and religion in the Middle East* (Lynne Rienner Publishers, 2007).

Digby Swift is Senior Education Adviser for the Middle East and North Africa (MENA) with the British Government Department for International Development (DfID). DfID supports disadvantaged countries and communities, for example in Yemen, and partners others in the region to tackle poverty on a regional and global scale. Dr Swift was for two years co-chair of the Education Task Force of the

G8-Broader Middle East and North Africa Partnership for Progress. This is now looking at education and the labour market. Previous work with DfID focused on Africa and included a three-year secondment to the European Commission. Dr Swift has taught in schools and universities in the UK and Africa. As head of Physics of Kenyatta University he started an Appropriate Technology Centre to bias university research and teaching to the needs of poorer communities. He has written a number of publications on physics, materials science and education, many linked to international development.

Bibliography

Abd al-Rahman, Abdullah, *The Emirates in the Memory of its Children*, Dubai 1990 (in Arabic).

Abdelkarim, Abbas and Haan, Hans, 'Skills and Training in the UAE: the need for and the dimensions of institutional intervention', in *Policy Research Papers*, no. 5, Dubai: Centre for Labour Market Research and Information, 2002.

——, 'Establishing a Labour Market Information System in the UAE: understanding the needs and identifying structures', in *Policy Research Papers*, no. 9, Dubai: Centre for Labour Market Research and Information, 2002.

Abdullah, Muhammad Morsy, *The United Arab Emirates: a modern history*, London: Croom Helm, 1978.

Abu Baker, Albadr, 'Political Economy of State Formation: the United Arab Emirates in comparative perspective', PhD Dissertation, University of Michigan, 1995.

Almolla Abdullah, F. H., 'Higher Education in Bahrain', paper presented at the Sixth Conference of the College of Education in the University of Bahrain, 'Higher Education and Development Requirements: a futuristic perspective', 20–22 November 2007, Kingdom of Bahrain, Sakheer, 2007 (in Arabic).

Altbach, Philip G., 'Education and Neocolonialism', in B. Ashcroft, G. Griffiths, and H. Tiffin, eds, *The Post-Colonial Studies Reader*, London and New York: Routledge, 2005.

Armbrust, Walter, *Mass Culture and Modernism in Egypt*, Cambridge: Cambridge University Press, 1996.

Bashshur, Munir, *Higher Education in the Arab States*, Beirut: UNESCO Office, 2004.

Bell, Gertrude, *Review of the Civil Administration of Mesopotamia*, London: His Majesty's Stationery Office, 1920.

Berkey, Jonathan P., 'Madrasas Medieval and Modern: politics, education, and the problem of Muslim identity', in Robert W. Hefner and Muhammad Qasim Zaman, eds., *Schooling Islam: the culture and politics of modern Muslim education*, Princeton, NJ: Princeton University Press, pp. 40–60.

Central Informatics Organisation (CIO), 'Bahrain in Numbers, Statistics of 2001', 2007, retrieved 22 October 2007 from the world wide web: http://www.cio.gov.bh/default.asp?action=article&id=190

——, 'Bahrain in Numbers, Statistics of 2004', 2007, retrieved 22 October 2007 from the world wide web: http://www.cio.gov.bh/pdf/stat2004.pdf

Champion, Daryl, *The Paradoxical Kingdom: Saudi Arabia and the momentum of reform*, New York: Columbia University Press, 2003.

Chatty, Dawn, 'Women Working in Oman: individual choice and cultural constraints', in *International Journal of Middle East Studies*, no. 32, 2000, pp. 241–54.

Coffman, James, 'Higher Education in the Gulf: privatization and Americanization', in *International Higher Education*, no. 33, 2003, pp. 17–19.

Davidson, Christopher M., *The United Arab Emirates: a study in survival*, Boulder and London: Lynne Rienner Publishers, 2005.

Dearing, R., *The National Committee of Inquiry into Higher Education (Dearing Report)*, London: HMSO, 1997.

Dekmejian, Richard H., 'Saudi Arabia's Consultative Council', in *Middle East Journal*, no. 52, 1998, pp. 204–18.

Delaney, Carol, *The Seed and the Soil: gender and cosmology in Turkish village society*, Berkeley: University of California Press, 1991.

Doumato, Eleanor Andella, 'Education in Saudi Arabia: gender, jobs, and the price of religion', in E. A. Doumato and M. P. Posusney, eds, *Women and Globalization in the Arab Middle East*, Boulder: Lynne Rienner Publishers, 2003, pp. 239–57.

Doumato, Eleanor A. and Starrett, Gregory, eds., *Teaching Islam: textbooks and religion in the Middle East*, Boulder: Lynne Rienner Publishers, 2007.

Economic Development Board, *Teaching is an Important Sector of Reform Projects in the Kingdom of Bahrain*, Manama, Kingdom of Bahrain: Economic Development Board, 2005 (in Arabic).

——, *Universities Inspections Project Briefing Package Improving Education and*

Training in the Kingdom of Bahrain, Manama, Kingdom of Bahrain: Economic Development Board, 2007.

——, *Universities Quality Review Project Overview Quality Assurance and Self-evaluation for Universities*, Manama, Kingdom of Bahrain: Economic Development Board, 2007 (in Arabic).

Encarta, 'Bahrain Facts and Figures', retrieved 19 October 2007 from the world wide web: http://Encarta.msn.com/fact_631504720/ Bahrain_facts_and_figures.html.

Ener, Mine, *Managing Egypt's Poor and the Politics of Benevolence, 1800–1952*, Princeton, NJ: Princeton University Press, 2003.

al-Fahim, Muhammad, *From Rags to Riches: a story of Abu Dhabi*, London: Arabian Publishing Ltd, 1995.

Fenelon, Kevin, *The United Arab Emirates: an economic and social survey*, London: Longman's Green & Co., 1973.

Fortna, Benjamin C., *Imperial Classroom: Islam, the state, and education in the late Ottoman empire*, Oxford: Oxford University Press, 2000.

Gambetta, Diego, and Hertog, Steffen, 'Engineers of Jihad', Sociology Working Papers number 2007-10, Department of Sociology, University of Oxford, 2007.

Goodman, Jane, *Berber Culture on the World Stage: from village to video*, Bloomington: Indiana University Press, 2005.

Halloran, William F., 'Zayed University: a new model for higher education', in *Education and the Arab World*, pp. 323–30.

Hamdan, Amani, 'Women and Education in Saudi Arabia: challenges and achievements', in *International Education Journal*, no. 6, 2005, pp. 42–54.

Hannerz, Ulf, 'The Neo-Liberal Culture Complex and Universities: a case for urgent anthropology?' in *Anthropology Today*, vol. 23, no. 5, 2007.

Hawley, Donald, *The Trucial States*, London: Allen & Unwin, 1970.

Heard-Bey, Frauke, *From Trucial States to United Arab Emirates,* London: Longman, 1996.

Higher Education Council (HEC), *Academic and Administrative By-laws*, Issa Town, Kingdom of Bahrain: Higher Education Council, 2007 (in Arabic).

——, *Building By-laws*, Issa Town, Kingdom of Bahrain: Higher Education Council, 2007 (in Arabic).

——, *Financial By-laws*, Issa Town, Kingdom of Bahrain: Higher Education Council, 2007 (in Arabic).

——, *Regulations Standards and Conditions of Licensure of Higher Education Institutes By-laws*, Issa Town, Kingdom of Bahrain: Higher Education Council, 2007 (in Arabic).

Hoodfar, Homa, *Between Marriage and the Market: intimate politics and survival in Cairo*, Berkeley: University of California Press, 1997.

Horowitz, Helen Lefkowitz, *Campus Life: undergraduate cultures from the end of the eighteenth century to the present*, New York: Knopf, 1987.

Ismael, Jacqueline S., *Kuwait: dependency and class in a rentier state*, Gainesville: University of Florida Press, 1993.

Kapiszewski, Andrzej, *Nationals and Expatriates: population and labour dilemmas of the Gulf Cooperation Council states*, Reading: Ithaca Press and Garnet, 2001.

al-Khalili, K. Y., 'Quality Assurance at the University of Bahrain', paper presented at Methods and Approaches to Institutional Audit Seminar, organised by the British Council, Kuwait, 14–17 January 2007.

Krieger, Zvika, 'Desert Boom', in *The Chronicle of Higher Education*, vol. 54, no. 29, 28 March 2008.

al-Lamki, Salma, 'The Development of Private Higher Education in the Sultanate of Oman: perception and analysis', in *International Journal of Private Education*, no. 1, 2006, pp. 54–77. Accessible online at http://www.xaiu.edu.cn/xaiujournal.

Lefrere, Paul, 'Competing Higher Education Futures in a Globalising World', in *European Journal of Education*, no. 42, 2007, pp. 201–12.

Lewis, Bernard, *Islam: From the Prophet Muhammad to the Capture of Constantinople, vol. II: Religion and Society*, Oxford: Oxford University Press, 1974.

Lorimer, John G., *Gazetteer of the Persian Gulf, Oman, and Central Arabia*, Superintendent Government Printing, part 1, *Historical*, part 2, *Geographical and Statistical*, Calcutta, 1908.

Luciani, Giacomo and Neugart, Felix, eds, *The EU and the GCC: a new partnership*, Munich: Bertelsmann Foundation, 2005.

Maawdeh, A., Hamoud, N., al-Khalifa, W. and al-Tahmazi, A., *Academic*

Programmes Offered by Licensed and Unlicensed Private Higher Education Institutes, Issa Town, Kingdom of Bahrain: Higher Education Council, 2007 (in Arabic).

Mazawi, André Elias, 'The Academic Workplace in Arab Gulf Public Universities', in P. G. Altbach, ed., *The Decline of the Guru: the academic profession in developing and middle-income countries*, New York: Palgrave Macmillan, 2003, pp. 231–69.

——, 'Divisions of Academic Labor: nationals and non-nationals in Arab Gulf universities', in *International Journal of Contemporary Sociology*, no. 40, 2003, pp. 91–110.

——, 'Contrasting Perspectives on Higher Education Governance in the Arab States', in *Higher Education: handbook of theory and research*, no. 20, 2005, pp. 133–18.

——, 'The Academic Profession in a Rentier State: the case of the Saudi Arabian professoriate', in *Minerva: a review of science, learning and policy*, no. 43, 2005, pp. 221–44.

——, 'State Power, Faculty Recruitment and the Emergence of Constituencies in Saudi Arabia', in R. Griffin, ed., *Education in the Muslim World: different perspectives – an overview*, Oxford: Symposium Books, 2006, pp. 55–78.

——, 'Besieging the King's Tower? En/gendering academic opportunities in the Gulf Arab states', in C. Brock and L. Zia Levers, eds, *Aspects of Education in the Middle East and North Africa*, Oxford: Symposium Books, 2007, pp. 77–97.

Mead, Margaret, 'Our Educational Emphases in Primitive Perspective', in *American Journal of Sociology*, vol. 48, no. 6, 1943, pp. 633–9.

Mellahi, Kamel, 'Human Resource Development through Vocational Education in Gulf Cooperation Countries: the case of Saudi Arabia', in *Journal of Vocational Education and Training*, no. 52, 2000, pp. 329–44.

Messick, Brinkley, *The Calligraphic State: textual domination and history in a Muslim society*, Berkeley: University of California Press, 1993.

Ministry of Education, 'The Royal Decree of Higher Education Council no. 3, 2005', Issa Town, Kingdom of Bahrain: Ministry of Education, 2005 (in Arabic).

Mohamed, Amel Ahmed Hassan, 'Distance Higher Education in the Arab

Region: the need for quality assurance frameworks', in *Online Journal of Distance Learning Administration*, no. 3, 2005.

Mottahedeh, Roy, *The Mantle of the Prophet: religion and politics in Iran*, Oxford: OneWorld Press, 2000.

Murphy, Emma, 'Agency and Space: the political impact of information technologies in the Gulf Arab states', in *Third World Quarterly*, no. 27, 2006, pp. 1059–83.

al-Musfir, Muhammad Salih, 'The United Arab Emirates: an assessment of federalism in a developing polity', PhD Dissertation, State University of New York at Binghamton, 1985.

Mutawwa, Muhammad A., *Development and Social Change in the Emirates*, Beirut, 1991 (in Arabic).

Muysken, Joan and Nour, Samia, 'Deficiencies in Education and Poor Prospects for Economic Growth in the Gulf Countries: the case of the UAE', in *Journal of Development Studies*, no. 42, 2006, pp. 957–80.

al-Nabeh, Najat Abdullah, 'The United Arab Emirates: regional and global dimensions', PhD Dissertation, Claremont Graduate School, 1984.

Nelson, C., 'Public and Private Politics: women in the Middle Eastern world', in *American Ethnologist*, 1973, pp. 551–63.

Nowaira, Amira, 'Lost and Found', in W. M. Hutchins, ed., *Egyptian Tales and Short Stories of the 1970s and 1980s*, Cairo: American University in Cairo Press, 1987, pp. 109–12.

O'Connell, James and Whitby, Simon, 'Constructing and Operating a Department of Peace Studies at the University of Bradford: a reflection on experience between 1973 and 1995', http://www.brad.ac.uk/acad/peace/about/history.pdf.

Onley, James, *The Arabian Frontier of the British Raj: merchants, rulers, and the British in the nineteenth-century Gulf*, Oxford: Oxford University Press, 2007.

Perthes, Völker, 'America's "Greater Middle East" and Europe: key issues for dialogue', in *Middle East Policy*, no. 11, 2004, pp. 85–97.

Quality Assurance Agency for Higher Education, *Higher Quality*, 2 and 3, 1997, www.qaa.ac.uk.

al-Rasheed, Madawi, *Contesting the Saudi State: Islamic voices from a new generation,* Cambridge: Cambridge University Press, 2007.

al-Rawaf, Haya Saad and Simmons, Cyril, 'Distance Higher Education for Women in Saudi Arabia: present and proposed', in *Distance Education*, no. 13, 1992, pp. 65–80.

Reid, Donald M., *Cairo University and the Making of Modern Egypt*, Cambridge: Cambridge University Press, 1990.

Ringer, Monica M., *Education, Religion, and the Discourse of Cultural Reform in Qajar Iran*, Costa Mesa, CA: Mazda Publishers, 2001.

Roberts, David, 'The Consequences of the Exclusive Treaties: a British view', in B. Pridham, ed., *The Arab Gulf and the West*, New York: St Martin's Press, 1985.

al-Rumaithi, Muhammad G., 'The Mode of Production in the Arab Gulf before the Discovery of Oil', in Tim Niblock, ed., *Social and Economic Development in the Arab Gulf*, London: Croom Helm, 1980.

al-Sayegh, Fatma, 'Merchants' Role in a Changing Society: The Case of Dubai, 1900–1990', in *Middle Eastern Studies*, vol. 34, no. 1, 1996.

Shaker, S. H., 'Distance Education in Bahrain: Situation and Needs', in *Open Learning*, no. 15, 2000, pp. 57–70.

Shalaba, Ahmad, *History of Muslim Education*, Beirut: Dar al-Kashshaf, 1954.

Shaw, K. E., ed., *Higher Education in the Gulf: problems and prospects*, Exeter: University of Exeter Press, 1997.

Soffan, L. U., *The Women of the United Arab Emirates,* London: Croom Helm, 1980.

Starrett, Gregory, *Putting Islam to Work: education, politics, and religious transformation in Egypt*, Berkeley: University of California Press, 1998.

——, 'When Theory is Data: coming to terms with "culture" as a way of life', in Melissa J. Brown, ed., *Explaining Culture Scientifically*, Seattle: University of Washington Press, 2008.

al-Sulayti, Hamad, 'Education and Training in the GCC Countries: some issues of concern', in *Education and the Arab World: challenges of the next millennium*, Abu Dhabi: The Emirates Centre for Strategic Studies and Research, 2000, pp. 271–8.

Swift, Digby, *Physics for Rural Development*, Oxford: John Wiley 1983.

UAE Ministry of Higher Education and Scientific Research, *Funding Students*

First: access to quality higher education programs in the United Arab Emirates, Abu Dhabi, 2004.

——, *Higher Education and the Future of the UAE*, Abu Dhabi, 2004.

——, *Educating the Next Generation of Emiratis: a master plan for UAE higher education*, Abu Dhabi, 2007.

UAE National Admissions and Placement Office, *Third Annual Survey of the No Shows*, Abu Dhabi, 2004.

UN, *United Nations Common Database*, Population total (UN Population Division's annual estimates and projections), ESDS International, Mimas, University of Manchester, updated in December 2007, accessed in March 2008. (http://www.esds.ac.uk)

UNDP, *Arab Human Development Report 2003: building a knowledge society*, United Nations Development Programme, Regional Bureau for Arab States, Amman: National Press, 2003.

UNESCO, *World Declaration on Higher Education for the Twenty-first Century: vision and action and framework for priority action for change and development in higher education*, adopted by the World Conference on Higher Education: Higher Education in the Twenty-First Century: Vision and Action, Paris: UNESCO, 9 October 1998.

United Arab Emirates Yearbook, Dubai, 2007.

University of North Carolina Tomorrow Commission, *Final Report*, Chapel Hill, NC: University of North Carolina General Administration, 2008.

Van Der Meulen, Hendrik, 'The Role of Tribal and Kinship Ties in the Politics of the United Arab Emirates', PhD Dissertation, Fletcher School of Law and Diplomacy, 1997.

Waardenburg, Jean-Jacques, *Les Universités dans le monde arabe actuel*, vols I & II, Paris: La Haye, 1966.

Walters, Timothy N., Kadragic, Alma and Walters, Lynne M., 'Miracle or Mirage: is development sustainable in the United Arab Emirates?', in *The Middle East Review of International Affairs*, no. 10, 2006, pp. 77–91.

Watson, D., *What Happened to the Dearing Report?*, London: Institute of Education, 2007.

Weber, Max, 'The Nature of Charismatic Domination', in W. G. Runciman, ed., *Weber: selections in translation*, Cambridge: Cambridge University Press, pp. 226–50.

Wilkins, Stephen, 'Human Resource Development through Vocational Education in the United Arab Emirates: the case of Dubai Polytechnic', in *Journal of Vocational Education and Training*, no. 54, 2002, pp. 5–26.

World Bank, *Knowledge Assessment Methodology*, KEI and KI Indexes, 2007. Updated in August 2007, accessed in March 2008. Permalink: http://go.worldbank.org/JGAO5XE940.

World Bank, *The Road Not Traveled: education reform in the Middle East and North Africa*. MENA Development Report, Washington DC: The World Bank, 2008. Permalink: http://go.worldbank.org/JLMVUoI6Ro.

World Bank, *World Development Indicators*, 2007, November 2007 edition, ESDS International, Mimas, University of Manchester, accessed in March 2008. http://www.esds.ac.uk.

Index

Mackenzie Smith, Peter 9–22, 172
Makerere University, Uganda 165–6
Mani bin Rashid Al Maktum, Shaikh 30
Mazawi, Dr André Elias 19–20, 59–72, 172
Mead, Margaret 88
Mellahi, Kamel 64
MENA countries (Middle East and North Africa)
    education reform framework 45, 50–2
    labour markets 45–6, 52–5
    socio-economic returns 44–6, 47–8
Michigan State University 118
Mohamed, Amel Ahmed Hassan 66
Mottahedeh, Roy 86
Muhammad Ali, Pasha 79, 83
Muhammad bin Rashid Al Maktum, Shaikh 127
Muhammad bin Saud, Shaikh 33
mutawa'a system (Qur'anic education) 25, 29, 144

Nahayan bin Mubarak Al Nahayan, Shaikh 112
Najd scientists 25
Nasser, President Jamal Abdul 35
National Bank of Dubai 127
New York Institute of Technology 13, 100
North Carolina, University of 84

Open University Validation Services (OUVS) 93, 94
al-Otaibi, Khalaf 26

Paris–Sorbonne, Abu Dhabi 13, 62, 100
Pasha, Dr Alwi 83
pearl fishing 25–6, 27–8, 139
Petroleum Institute, Abu Dhabi 18, 99
private institutions 19, 20, 52, 62–3, 93, 100, 122–3
    Bahrain 137–8, 140–1

Al-Qasimi School, Sharjah 27, 32
Qatar Education City 19, 64

Qatar Foundation 62, 84
quality assurance systems 10, 14, 16, 94–5, 123, 140–2
quality of higher education 13–14, 51–2, 116–17, 119–20

Ra's al-Khaimah 25, 33
Rashid bin Said Al Maktum, Shaikh 31
The Road not Travelled, World Bank 9–10, 42–56
Rolls Royce International 127, 129

Said bin Maktum Al Maktum, Shaikh 29, 30, 31
Sa'id Pasha 86
Al-Salmya School, Dubai 27
Saudi Arabia, state provision 62–3, 66–7
Saudi British Electronic Institute, Riyadh 18
Shah of Iran 33
Shakhbut bin Sultan Al Nahayan, Shaikh 33–4
Shalaby, Ahmad 75
al-Shamlan, Professor Ali 16–17, 149–57, 172–3
Spencer, Herbert 82
Starrett, Professor Gregory 11–12, 73–91, 173
student numbers (2003) 59
Sulayman Pasha 77–8
Sultan bin Khalifa Al Nahayan, Shaikh 107
Swift, Dr Digby 16, 158–67, 173–4

Tattersall, Arthur 165
Al-Tatweerya School, Sharjah 27

UK Quality Assurance Agency 14, 94
UNDP, *Arab Human Development Report* 19, 42
UNESCO, *World Declaration on Higher Education* 42
United Arab Emirates (UAE)
    economic role of women 103–4
    Educating the Next Generation of

About the London Middle East Institute

The London Middle East Institute (LMEI) of SOAS is a charitable, tax-exempt organisation whose purpose is to promote knowledge of all aspects of the Middle East, both among the general public and to those with special interests in the region. Drawing on the expertise of over seventy SOAS academic Middle East specialists, accessing the substantial library and other resources of SOAS, and interacting with over 300 individual and corporate affiliates, the LMEI since its founding in 2002 has sponsored conferences, seminars and exhibitions; conducted training programmes; and undertaken consultancies for public and private sector clients. The LMEI publishes a monthly magazine – *The Middle East in London* – and with Saqi it publishes four books annually in the SOAS Middle East Issues series. These activities are guided by a Board of Trustees on which is represented SOAS, the British Academy, the University of London, the Foreign and Commonwealth Office and private sector interests.

Professor Robert Springborg
MBI Chair in Middle East Studies
Director, London Middle East Institute
School of Oriental and African Studies
Russell Square, London WC1H 0XG
United Kingdom
www.lmei.soas.ac.uk